How I Sold My House
in Six Days
on Craigslist

And Saved Almost $5,000 with My
Simple Online "For Sale By Owner" Marketing Plan

By Jonni Good

Wet Cat Books, Brookings, South Dakota

Published by Wet Cat Books
Brookings, SD 57006
Contact: *jonni@wetcatbooks.com*

The digital portrait of the author on the cover is by Jessie Rasche: *http://jessiesfineart.com*

Printed and bound in USA

Good, Jonni, 1949-
    How I Sold My House in Six Days on Craigslist: And Saved Almost $5,000 with My Simple Online "For Sale By Owner" Marketing Plan
ISBN 978-0-9741065-6-4

Business & Investing/Real Estate/Buying & Selling Homes

Please Note: The author is not a real estate agent, attorney or accountant. The opinions expressed in this book often run counter to the usual "expert" advice, and are based solely on the author's own personal experience in selling her own homes. If you need professional advice, please contact a good real estate attorney or a local broker.

The author is not associated in any way with *Craigslist.org.*

Contents

My Whirlwind
House-Selling Adventure

IN THE MIDDLE of June, 2012, I suddenly realized that I needed to sell my house, and I needed to sell it fast. I spent the next three weeks sprucing the place up. Then, on Saturday, July 7, my Craigslist ad went online.

Two days later, on July 9, I showed the house to a *very* interested young lady who teaches third grade at the local elementary school. Her parents came with her, because they were helping their daughter buy her first home. She told me she needed to talk to her loan officer at the mortgage company, but she loved the house and she'd be back in a few days. She begged me to let her know if anyone made an offer before she came back.

I wrote my daughter an email that night. The subject line said "I think I sold my house!"

The buyer returned on Friday, July 13, and we sat down at the kitchen table to fill in the paperwork. She didn't quibble about the price, and she agreed to pay for any repairs that might be required by her bank. The most difficult part of the "negotiation" was figuring out what to write in the blanks on the purchase agreement form.

Another buyer had scheduled an appointment to see the house on Saturday, so I called him up and told him the house had sold.

About 40 days later, the buyer's mortgage was finalized, I got my check, and the moving van arrived.

It almost felt a bit *too* fast, but I couldn't have hoped for a better outcome. My buyer was pre-qualified for her loan, she paid my asking price, and I didn't have to pay a huge real estate commission. Even more importantly, I was able to get most of the equity out of the house just before local home prices started to go down.

Why I decided to sell

I'd been watching the real estate market and the financial news for a long time, because it just happens to interest me. In fact, during the real estate bubble, back in 2006, this particular quirk of mine helped me realize that it was time to sell my previous house, in Portland, Oregon.

At that time, most people still had themselves convinced that home prices would keep going up forever, even though prices had already started to go down in many cities. The public was still unaware of the looming sub-prime mortgage crisis, and the Lehman Brothers bankruptcy was still two years away. However, in May of 2006, CNNMoney.com posted an article titled *Real Estate Cools Down*. The article began with this bad news:

> *Real estate gains came to an abrupt halt in the first quarter of 2006, with the median price of a U.S. home falling 3.3 percent from the fourth quarter of 2005 ...*

I knew I had to sell my little Portland house in order to hold on to its inflated equity. I listed the house with a local real estate agent, and it sold within two weeks for almost twice as much as I paid for it three years earlier. I took the profit from that house and moved to the small eastern Oregon city of La Grande, Oregon. That's when I bought the house that I recently sold on Craigslist.

As soon as I moved into my new home, I started fixing the place up. I didn't spend much money, but I installed some new laminated flooring from Ikea, and I replaced a wall that a previous owner had taken out, which gave me two bedrooms instead of one. Mostly, though, I spent my time digging up the grass, putting in a huge garden, adding a (slightly illegal) chicken run, and planting fruit trees. I had wonderful neighbors who watched my crazy urban farming projects with amusement, and they never complained about my front-yard potatoes or the clucking of my hens.

I still occasionally went online and checked the local real estate listings. Home prices in our small city didn't go down much, even though national home prices kept falling in the six years after the collapse of the housing bubble. However, every time I looked at the listings on the real estate websites, I saw the same houses. While the listing prices weren't going down, the market was very slow, and very few houses seemed to be changing hands, in spite of the record-low mortgage interest rates.

I also had an opportunity to see the real estate market up close and personal. My home business, as a web publisher and craft book author, gives me plenty of free time for taking long walks around the neighborhood with my dog Banjo, an aging mystery-mutt. Beginning in 2008, while we walked around town I couldn't help but notice that many of the houses in my neighborhood were going into foreclosure. The uncut grass is usually the first indication that something is wrong. Then you see a notice taped to the front door, and trash starts to pile up in the alley.

By 2012, there were 7 foreclosed homes within two blocks of my house. This naturally affected the feel of the neighborhood, and I nervously waited for the banks to start putting them up for sale. However, for reasons known only to the banks, the empty houses just sat there–in some cases, for years–without being put on the market.

Then, in June of 2012, that changed. Two foreclosed houses right down the street from me were listed at prices that were up to 45% less than their previous owners paid for them in 2006. One of these houses was very similar to the one I owned. At these deeply discounted prices, the foreclosed houses sold almost immediately, and I felt that I was watching my own equity disappearing into thin air.

Now that the banks had finally started to dump their foreclosures, home prices in the city would *have* to go down, just like they had already gone down almost everywhere else.

Now what?

First, I took three weeks to make the house look as good as possible. Then I started thinking about how I would advertise my house.

Since the market was so slow, and houses were sitting on the market for months, I wanted to make sure that my own house didn't suffer the same fate. I used my web-publishing experience to create an inexpensive ($22) online marketing plan, which included a free Craigslist ad and a super-basic WordPress website. I made sure that anyone who looked for a house on Craigslist would be able to find my ad, and that it would stand out from other ads on that site.

Of course, most of the houses that I was competing with were listed by local agents, and those houses weren't selling. I wanted to do better, so I focused my marketing effort on the specific potential buyers who would be most likely to fall in love with my house. To do that, I used the niche marketing techniques that I learned during the 12 years that I've been making my living online.

Like I said before, my house almost sold *too* quickly for me to be quite emotionally prepared for it. There was less than four weeks between making the decision to sell, and having a signed offer in hand. After my buyer saw my house that first time, I even thought about calling her up and telling her that I'd changed my mind before it was too late! I was feeling seller's remorse, and I hadn't even officially sold the house yet.

Fortunately, in the four days before the buyer and her parents came back and made their offer, I had time to calm down and reaffirm my belief that it was the right thing to do.

As I write this page, it is now December of the same year, and I just made an offer on my next home, in Brookings, South Dakota. In a few weeks I'll be moving out of my temporary rental house and into my new home. I'll be living within a few miles of my daughter and her family, four blocks from a fantastic library, and within walking distance of the cultural events at the local university and the cute downtown shops.

Unfortunately, I wasn't able to buy my new house directly from a seller, although I checked Craigslist every day. The only houses for sale in Brookings in the last few months have been listed with the local brokers, so I had to make my offer through a real estate agent.

Since I sold my own home so recently, I couldn't help but compare the two house-buying experiences from a seller's point of view—and now I'm even *more* convinced that if I ever decide to sell another house, I'll be selling it myself, on Craigslist.

What you'll find in this book

In this book I'll show you all the steps I took to get my home ready to sell, the ad I placed on Craigslist, and the easy website I created to back up the ad.

I know that some of my readers will now be asking–Why bother making a website? Why not just put an ad on Craigslist like everybody else?

And that, of course, is exactly the point. In a very slow real estate market, I knew I couldn't afford to do the same things that everyone else was doing. And, since I didn't have a real estate agent helping me, my ad had to give my potential buyers just as much information as they would normally get by surfing the local real estate websites or Zillow.com. You can't get that much information onto a Craigslist ad.

And yes, I know that many people start to hyperventilate at the very idea of trying to build a website, but it isn't hard–it's really just a matter of filling in a few blanks and uploading some pictures. In fact, it isn't much harder than posting an ad on Craigslist.org, which many people do every day. The few hours I spent building the website helped my Craigslist ad stand out from all the other ads on that site, and I'm convinced that my house would not have sold as quickly without it.

I'll also show you how I used my experience as a web publisher to write the ad and website to attract the buyers who would be most likely to actually want to my house, (and to make sure that I wouldn't have to show the house to anyone who *wouldn't* want to buy it). This is called *niche marketing,* and it's an important idea for anyone selling anything online. I'll explain this idea in more detail in the following chapters.

But remember ...

My methods helped me sell *my* house fast in a slow market. However, please don't consider this a blueprint for selling your own house. With real estate, location really does matter. So does the local economy, the kind of home you're selling, the sort of buyer who would be attracted to your home, the number of other similar homes currently available in the same area, and the prices people are getting for them. It also depends on how comfortable you are with the idea of selling your own house.

I'm not a real estate expert *or* a lawyer. You won't find any legal advice in this book, and I'm not going to tell you how to fill out the purchase agreement or any other legal contract. For that, you should hire a good real estate attorney. (Fortunately, attorneys are *way* cheaper than real estate agents!)

I also think it's important to remember that *every* real estate deal is stressful, for both buyers and sellers. It can't help but be stressful, because so much money changes hands and so many people are involved in the process, from the day the purchase agreement is signed to the day, perhaps several months later, when the deal finally closes. Selling my house without an agent didn't prevent *any* of that stress–it just helped me save some money.

Actually, it helped me save a whole *lot* of money.

I have sold other houses before (but never as a FSBO), and I was even a real estate agent once upon a time, (for a very *short* time, and it was many years ago). Those past experiences were certainly useful when it came to getting my house ready to sell and choosing the right price. However, it was really my recent experience as a web publisher that helped me find my buyer so quickly, with a free ad on Craigslist.

Why I Decided to Sell My House Without an Agent

A{s I just} mentioned, I sold real estate for a few months as an agent many years ago. Back then, I had a broker and his entire office to back me up. I remember that it was fun looking at all the houses that were for sale, and I liked meeting the people who were buying and selling them, but I couldn't handle the pressure of commission sales. I stayed in the real estate business for less than a year.

This time, I would be selling my house entirely on my own, and I was understandably nervous. Here's why I decided to give it a try, in spite of my natural concerns:

Reason #1. A friend recently sold her home without an agent, so I knew it was possible—even in a slow market

About 6 months before I decided to put my own house on the market, a friend of mine sold her home by putting an ad on Craigslist. Things worked out well for her, even though she'd never sold a house before—and she had no previous experience selling *anything* online.

It wasn't a stress-free experience, though. Sue's Craigslist ad was online for several months before she found a buyer. Once she did find a couple who wanted the house, she had to be flexible, because the buyers had some credit issues they needed to work out with the bank, and it took several more months before they could actually make their official offer. However, these same issues would have come up even if Sue had listed the house with an agent. Her personal relationship with the buyers helped keep the deal moving forward, in spite of some major stress points.

Since my friend was able to sell her home at the price she wanted, and at a time when very few houses were selling in our city, *and* she did it without paying a real estate agent, I figured I could do it, too.

Reason #2: I saved the 6% commission

When I sold a house back in 2006 at the top of the real estate bubble, I didn't think much about the added cost of the agent's commission. The profit I received from the sale more than made up for that extra 6%. In 2012, however, the situation was completely different.

As I mentioned in the last chapter, our local home prices held steady for a long time, but banks were finally starting to dump their foreclosures. With prices finally starting to drop, I knew I would be lucky to sell my home for the same price I'd paid for it six years earlier. Adding the cost of the commission on top of the home price might keep the house from selling at all.

According to Zillow.com, the median home values in La Grande, Oregon went down a whopping 20.6% in 2012, and almost *all* of this fall in prices happened in the second half of the year, after I sold my home. You can see the Zillow chart if you go to:

http://lagrandehouse.com/prices

When home prices are on the rise, the increased value will sometimes help you pay the real estate commission–just like when I sold a house back in 2006. In a falling market, though, that is much less likely.

The real estate commission, and the fees charged by the mortgage company, the title company, the appraisers and inspectors, etc., are all part of the cost of selling a house, but these fees don't add to the actual *value* of the house–they just add to the amount of money it costs you to sell. In a falling market, those fees can make a big difference in your bank balance after the house is sold.

I couldn't really avoid the closing costs and bank fees, but the real estate fee *could* be avoided if I sold my house myself. As an added bonus, eliminating the commission meant I could afford to offer some help to my buyers with their closing costs, and that helped make a quick sale possible.

You'll sometimes see an ad on Craigslist that goes something like this:

> *If my house isn't sold in 30 days*
> *I'll be listing it with an agent.*
> *That means you'll save $xxx if you buy the house now!*
> *Don't delay!*

Sorry, but that's not how it works. The agent's services don't add any value to the home. If the house is really worth $100,000 today, it won't be worth $106,000 next week, just because it's now being represented by an agent. And yes, the buyer's own agent is going to point this out to her clients when they're getting ready to make an offer, even though *you*, as the seller, will be paying that agent's commission. This doesn't seem entirely fair, but that's still the way it works.

Reason #3: Some real estate agents don't like cheap houses, and my house was the least expensive move-in-ready house on the market

I knew from past experience that most agents prefer, quite naturally, to sell expensive houses. This makes perfect sense, because agents are independent contractors who are in business for themselves. Like everyone else, they want to get paid as much as possible for their time. My house was not expensive—in fact, it was one of the least expensive move-in-ready houses in town.

I sold my house for about $78,000, while the "average" listing price for homes in my city at the time was $150,000, according to Zillow.com. A selling agent would receive $1,170 for selling my house—that's the 6% commission ($4,689), split four ways between buyer's agent, seller's agent, and two brokers. If the same agent sold a $150,000 house, she would be paid $2,250 instead, over $1,000 more for the same amount of work and time.

Another problem, from the point of view of an agent, is that cheaper houses appeal to first-time buyers—and that can mean more work for an agent because inexperienced buyers often need extra hand-holding during the long process of getting their loan, working with appraisers and inspectors, and all the nerve-wracking and seemingly unnecessary waiting time that causes so much confusion and stress.

In the past I *have* worked with some wonderful agents who specialized in selling homes to first-time home buyers—but I've also worked with agents who simply listed my inexpensive house and then never gave it another thought.

Reason #4: The Internet makes it easier to sell a house without an agent

In the past, real estate agents would see a house when it appeared on the multiple listing service, and then call up potential buyers to tell them about it. If their clients didn't like the first house they were shown, the agent would call them again when another appropriate house was listed.

Now it usually happens the other way around–buyers find a house on the Internet themselves, and then call an agent to make an appointment to see it.

In fact, many good agents will add their client's email address to a subscription to the local listings on Zillow.com, so the buyers are automatically notified every time another house goes on the market. This is good news for modern for-sale-by-owners, because buyers are already "trained" to find their own houses by looking through the listings shown online.

The Internet helps buyers as much as sellers, because everyone now has access to information they never had before. You can look on Zillow.com, or on any number of similar websites, and find almost every home currently for sale in your city–all shown on a convenient map. Many for-sale-by-owner houses are shown right alongside those offered by Century 21® and ReMax®. (I intended to add my own house to Zillow, but it sold before I got around to it.)

You can often see the amount of time the house has been for sale, and any changes that have been made to the listing price. You can (sometimes) see how much the current owners paid for the house, and when they bought it.

You can also find houses in the neighborhood that have recently sold, along with the selling price. This is a valuable piece of information for a seller, because listing prices can reflect a seller's hopes and unrealistic dreams, while the recent *sales* prices show what people have actually paid for houses in the neighborhood. This information makes it much easier to find the right price for a house before you put your ad in the paper or on Craigslist.org.

Although it isn't as helpful, you can see the assessed value set by the county for other houses in the neighborhood, and you can take notice of Zillow's estimate of the current market values (which is really only a computer-generated guess, and shouldn't be taken too seriously).

If you pay attention to the online real estate sites for a few months, you will know how many local houses are for sale, how much they're listed for, which ones are selling and which ones have been sitting there unsold for months (and sometimes, for years). You can tell if prices in the area are going down or up, and if foreclosures are currently being dumped on the market for a deep discount–which could help you determine if it's a good time to sell your house or if you should hold on to it a little longer. Someone who pays attention to this information can, within a few months, become almost as knowledgeable about the market as a seasoned agent.

All that information is now easily available online, but you aren't totally dependent on information you can find on your own. When my friend Sue started thinking about selling her house, she was nervous about setting the right price, and she still hadn't totally convinced herself that she had the skills she needed to sell the house herself. She called an agent she knew, and asked her if she'd be willing to come to the house and explain the services she offered. The agent was more than willing to do that. She took a look a the house, brought printouts of current and past listings, and helped Sue feel confident that her own assessment of the home's value was right. Although Sue decided not to hire the agent, she kept her number on hand in case she later changed her mind.

There was actually another option for us, half-way between total FSBO and hiring an agent. In our small city in Oregon there's a company that will provide a seller with all the necessary forms. They also put your house on their own website, along with the houses of their other clients. For an additional fee, they'll list your house with the local multiple listing service. (Of course, if you accept an offer submitted by an agent, the buyer will try to get you to pay their agent's commission, but it's usually cut in half if there's only one agent involved).

What this company *doesn't* do is show the house to potential buyers, or help you fill out the forms, or follow through with any of the people who are involved in the entire process of selling a home, like the mortgage bank and the escrow company. Sue and I both decided not to use their services, because you can buy the forms for a few dollars, and a Craigslist ad gets your house online for free.

Reason #5: The services provided by an agent are available elsewhere, at a lower cost

I've already discussed the fact that you can now get access to market information that was previously difficult to find without an agent—but agents do more than just help a seller determine a fair listing price for their home. For instance:

- Agents schedule showings so buyers can see the house;

- They help the buyer fill out the real estate purchase form;

- They explain the offer to the seller;

- They take the signed and accepted contracts to the escrow company, which orders the title report;

- They keep in contact with the mortgage company and escrow company, and they make any changes to the original purchase agreement that might be needed after the inspection and appraisal, and;

- The agent may offer suggestions about what inspector the buyers should hire, and they may even suggest mortgage companies and insurance agents.

Even though many of these services help the buyer rather than the seller, it's still the seller who pays the commission.

It may sound like a long list of services, but I decided that everything on that list could be handled without an agent. Here's how:

- **Showing the house:**

If the house isn't listed, the "scheduled showing" really just involves a potential buyer calling the number in the Craigslist ad, and showing up at the appointed time. My buyer called, and I showed her the house. Another buyer called, and I told him the house was already sold. That really didn't seem too hard.

Some people feel a bit nervous about letting strangers into their homes, especially if they live alone or if they have small, easily stolen valuables sitting around the house. If you do live by yourself and you're uncomfortable being in your house alone with a stranger, you can always ask a neighbor to come over just before the buyer is expected to arrive. If you have collectibles that someone could easily nab, you'll want to put them in a safe place even if you do have an agent–they can't possibly watch a buyer every minute they're in your house. Fortunately, I lived in a small city with a low crime rate and I don't own a lot of things that anyone would want to steal, so I was less worried about these issues than some people might need to be.

Real estate agents will tell you that buyers feel uncomfortable looking into closets and other personal spaces if the owner is in the house, so, (according to real estate agents), it's always better to let buyers see the house when the owner isn't home. That might be an issue for some people, but my buyer and her parents had no problem with "invading my space." After I showed them around, I could tell that they were honest and trustworthy, so I offered to let them look the place over while I busied myself somewhere else in the house. They got their privacy, and I got my sale.

- **The purchase form:**

The real estate purchase form (which is called different things in different states) only costs a few dollars. The local escrow company may sell them, and even if they don't, they should be able to direct you to a local bookstore or copy shop that does. The forms you buy will have all the same information that an agent's form contains, with almost all the same blanks the buyer needs to fill in when they make their offer. If you need more space to add special contingencies, you can use a blank piece of paper, as long as everyone signs it.

My buyer and her parents bought their form from the escrow company, and they filled out the purchase agreement at my kitchen table. Then they took it to a local attorney to make sure all the spaces were filled out correctly. The lawyer added a few words, and his time cost them about $50.

I actually felt much more confident about the paper I signed that day than I did five months later, when my real estate agent filled out the purchase agreement for the house I'm currently buying. Because so many additional forms are required by law when an agent helps someone buy a house, I sat there while he handed me page after page of legal "boilerplate." He explained each one quickly, and then pointed to the line where I should sign.

Most of the forms had nothing to do with the purchase, but simply informed me about things like lead paint and who the agent was representing. After many minutes of this, my brain started to turn off. I did notice when he accidentally wrote down an offering price that was $100,000 higher than it should have been, (whew!) but I didn't read the forms over as carefully as I should have—which is never a good idea when dealing with legal documents.

In contrast, when my buyers and I filled out the purchase form together at the kitchen table, the experience was more pleasant, it cost thousands of dollars less, and we actually made fewer mistakes.

- **The negotiations:**

Negotiating the sale between buyers and sellers is one of the primary services provided by an agent. In fact, when an agent is involved, the buyers and sellers of a house may never meet each other—all communication between the two parties is done in writing, and the signed offers and counter-offers are delivered back and forth by the selling agent and the listing agent. The buyers and sellers are carefully kept apart.

Back when I worked as a real estate agent, we were told to emphasize to potential sellers that these negotiations could be really difficult if the buyers and sellers ever sat down in the same room together. Supposedly, personal feelings would get hurt, emotions would take over, and deals would be lost because "amateurs" wouldn't be able to negotiate without messing everything up. I believed it for a while–until I met a great many real estate agents who have no special negotiating skills whatsoever.

I think negotiations *can* be tricky if one of the parties in the deal is a fast-talking real estate investor who's really good at getting the very best deal, while the other party is an individual with almost no experience in selling a home. In that instance, I'd want some help from a knowledgeable expert before signing *anything*–but you can hire this help from a good real estate attorney. An attorney's time is a good investment in any case. You pay the attorney *by the hour*, which costs considerably less than the commission you'd pay to a real estate agent, who has far less training.

And you *never* have to sign anything right away, while the buyer is still in the house. I knew that if someone offered less than I wanted for my house, I could always take their signed purchase agreement and tell them I'd need a few days to think it over. That didn't turn out to be needed, but it was still an option that helped me feel more comfortable.

I *did* do a bit of up-front work to make the negotiations go more easily, even before I met my buyer. For instance, I didn't start out asking for more money than I thought the house was worth, the way so many sellers do. They expect the buyer to offer less, and then buyer and seller go back and forth until they find a number they both agree to.

I really hate haggling. To prevent that scenario, I priced the house correctly from the beginning. Since my buyer had been paying just as much attention to local home prices on real estate sites as I had been, (she did find my house online, after all), she knew the price was fair and agreed to pay it without a quibble.

Of course, the price isn't the only thing that people have to agree on when a house is sold. My buyers were approved for a low-down FHA loan, and I knew that my house wouldn't pass an FHA appraisal without some minor repairs. I told the buyer during our first meeting that any repairs that were required by the bank would have to be done, *and paid for,* by the buyer–I just told them that I'm getting too old to climb a ladder to paint my eaves, and that I couldn't afford to pay for labor and materials. I made this clear the first time I met them, right while we were walking around the house. I even posted a list of things that would probably need to be fixed on my website, so my buyer knew the house wasn't "perfect" before she ever saw it.

The repairs got done (by the buyer's parents, as it turned out), and I didn't have to pay for them. I doubt that an agent could have negotiated a better deal than I did on my own–and the best part was that the buyers were just as happy about the deal as I was, because I made sure that there would be no surprises, right from the start.

- ● **After the Purchase Agreement is Signed:**

Once an agreement has been received and accepted, the buyer will write out an earnest money check for $500 or $1,000. The check and all the forms are then taken to the local escrow company. The buyer arranges for the home inspection and fills out an application for a loan. The escrow company arranges for the title report. If you have an agent, she would let the seller know when all these things have take place, but it's just as easy for the buyer and seller to keep each other informed by a phone call or email, instead.

My buyer handed me a check, we signed the paperwork, and I got on my bicycle and rode down to the escrow company, which happened to be right down the street. The escrow agent opened up a new account for me, she deposited the check in the escrow account, and she ordered the initial title report. She certainly didn't mind that the paperwork was delivered by me instead of an agent.

The buyer chooses an inspector, and the two agents involved usually schedule a time when the inspector can get into the house. If there aren't any agents involved, the buyer just calls up an inspector herself, and then calls the owner to make sure he can get in. (In my case, the buyer's mortgage company recommended that she hire the inspector even before she made the offer, so he was looking around the basement and snooping into the bedrooms while the buyer filled out the purchase agreement. I've never seen that done before, but it seemed to work out just fine.)

The appraisal will be scheduled by the bank, and the appraiser will let the seller know when they need access to the house. After the inspection and the appraisal, it's often necessary to do some more negotiations if there are any problems that the buyer didn't know about when they agreed to buy the house, but, as I said, we had agreed ahead of time that the buyers would be responsible for any problems that showed up on these reports, so we didn't have to bother with more paperwork.

When my friend Sue sold her house, she spent quite a lot of time talking with a loan officer at the local bank so that she could, in turn, help her buyers find a way to make their mortgage work in spite of their credit problems. My own buyer didn't need any help from me, because she had been working with a bank for weeks before she found a house she wanted, and she had already been pre-approved for a loan.

After the deal was signed, my buyer's loan officer was more than happy to talk to me every time I called. I knew when the appraisal was scheduled, when the paperwork was sent to underwriting, and when they needed the buyer to send them an additional form.

One of an agent's primary services is following through with all the people involved after the offer is accepted, but, at least in my case, working without agents didn't cause any problems at all, and everything got done on time.

Reason #6: The seller pays the buyer's agent, who works against the seller's own interests

Several years ago, some changes were made by state real estate boards to help buyers feel more confident working with agents. In the past, some buyers complained that they thought an agent was working for *them* when, in fact, at that time *every* agent was working for the seller. This confusion would sometimes work against the buyer's interest. For instance, the buyer might tell the agent how much money he was willing to pay if his first offer was turned down, and the agent would give this information to the seller without the buyer's knowledge.

Now, though, the agent who actually finds a buyer and does the work of selling a listed house must promise to work *only* for the buyer, unless the agent is both the listing agent and the selling agent. My current agent even asked me to sign an "Exclusive Buyer's Contract." This form is essentially a legal promise that I would only buy a house through that agent. (I still haven't figured out how this contract serves the interests of either buyer or seller, but it seems to be standard procedure with all the agents in town.) This means that the selling agent has a strong commitment to their client, the *buyer*, and they take this relationship seriously.

A selling agent isn't particularly interested in selling *your* house, because they have lots of houses to choose from, and they show the houses that they think will be easiest to sell.

A selling agent will work hard to get the lowest price for their client, *not* the best price for the seller.

And a selling agent will try to negotiate the greatest number of other advantages, like seller-paid repairs, for their client.

This means that a seller might end up paying a large commission to a selling agent who has actively worked against the seller's own interests—since that's exactly what they're *supposed* to do, now that buyers have a right to expect an agent to work for them exclusively.

The listing agent *does* work for the seller, and will look out for the seller's interests when an offer is presented—or at least she should, since that's what she's being paid to do.

The situation was completely different when I put an ad on Craigslist and sold my home *without* an agent. When I made the appointment with a buyer to see my house, *my* house was the only one I showed to her. My buyer wanted to take a few days to think it over, so I made another appointment for her to come back and see *my* house again—I didn't make arrangements to show her the house down the street. Then we came to a mutually-beneficial agreement, without anyone putting any roadblocks in our way.

Not only did it work out just fine for all of us, but it was a more pleasant experience, too. I got to meet the person who would be living in my house after I moved out. She visited a few times while we waited for the house to close, and I sent her home with some of the grapes and corn in the garden. She said hello to the kids on the block, who, as it turned out, would be in her elementary class in the fall, and I introduced her to her new next-door neighbors.

In spite of the stress that's always involved in selling a house, I walked away feeling really good about the way things turned out, and that's worth a lot to me.

The fact that I saved almost $5,000 made it even better.

Getting Ready

As soon as I decided that it was time to sell my house, I rented a dumpster and threw away all the "stuff" in the garage and basement that I hadn't used in years, and I took a few garbage bags full of bottles and cans back to the store for my refund.

A few pieces of furniture were moved around to make the living room feel less cramped, and I generally picked up and rearranged things around the house. I also made sure the chicken run was nice and clean, and I gave away my chickens, (but I should have kept them–it turned out that my buyer was really excited about having chickens in her back yard, and she hoped to bring her third-grade students on a field trip to visit her new flock. However, I'm sure she'll enjoy picking out the new chicks next spring at the local farm supply store).

Once all the clutter was gone, I repainted the front door to make the house feel more welcoming from the outside, and I added a coat of paint to the front bedroom, living room and kitchen, so the house would look fresh and inviting on the inside, too.

As you can tell if you look at the photos on my webpage, (*LaGrandeHouse.com*) I didn't do much to "stage" the house, and I certainly didn't go out and buy new furniture so the place would look nicer. In fact, I spent less than $300 on paint and dumpster fees to get ready to sell my house.

During the six years when I lived in the home, I updated the bathroom, I added new flooring in the living room, and I put back that wall that the previous owner had taken out. However, I made these changes to make the house more comfortable for *me*, not for the people who would live there next.

My unconventional opinions about "staging" a house

If you take a look at my website, the first thing you'll notice is color–and lots of it. I've been using essentially the same wall colors for the last three houses that I've sold, and it really seems to help, even though my colors don't appear in most of the "expert" articles about staging a house.

My theory is fairly simple–I get a house ready to sell the same way I would get it ready if I was expecting a very important guest. I would naturally want the house to look its best, but *I'm* still the one living there–and I've learned from experience that you never know how long it will take to sell a house after the sign goes up and the ads are posted.

I would never go out and rent furniture to make the house look better, like some people do. I also wouldn't put my family photos (or my daughter's paintings, or my sculptures, or my books), in storage, just because they might not appeal to a buyer's tastes. I definitely wouldn't plow up the vegetable garden and replant the grass, even though I knew that very few people were looking for a small urban farm.

When the owner's personality is removed from a house, the house itself loses some of its own character, and I think that actually makes it *harder* to sell a house.

This might be a good place for me to tell you a short story from years past. When I lived in Spokane, Washington, about fifteen years ago, I owned a small house that I wanted very badly to sell. Before looking for a listing agent, I started reading articles about how to "stage" a house, and they all gave similar advice. In fact, you've probably read many of the same articles, or ones just like them.

- Paint the walls white, they said, so I painted the walls white.

- Use neutral colors, they said, so I had beige carpeting installed (terrible choice for someone with two large dogs and a muddy garden).

- Remove all family photos and any artwork that might keep buyers from imagining themselves in the house, they said—so that's exactly what I did.

It no longer looked like *my* house, but it looked the way the articles told me it *had* to look if I wanted buyers to like it.

Then I listed the house.

My real estate agent didn't show the house to *anyone* before the listing ran out. I listed it again, with a different agent, and I got the same response. About *two years* went by, with nothing changing except the name of the real estate company on the sign out front.

I finally gave up and went to the paint store. I bought the highly-saturated earth colors that I love. (By then, I assumed that I'd be in the house forever, so I might as well enjoy it.) I painted the walls, hung up my photos and paintings, and then called another realtor. She loved the house, and she sold it within a month.

Coincidence? Maybe. Or maybe not. Without any kind of scientific study, I can't know for sure.

However, I used the same colors on the walls of my tiny house in Portland, and it sold two weeks after it was listed. But, to be fair, my little 480 square foot house *was* the least expensive move-in-ready house on the market at that time. That may have been why it sold so quickly, or perhaps it was because I hired a real estate agent who actually lived in the neighborhood and who specialized in first-time home buyers.

I used the same colors on the house I recently sold on Craigslist (adding the turquoise in the kitchen, a new color for me). This house sold in 6 days—but, again, to be fair, most of the similar houses in town were listed at least $20,000 higher. Those houses had been on the market for months, so they were obviously overpriced, and some of them needed extensive repairs or updating to make them appealing to buyers.

But my buyer *did* fall in love with that turquoise kitchen and the huge vegetable garden.

Can the wrong color make the house harder to sell?

In spite of my strong opinions about color (I'm an artist in real life, so that's only natural), I *do* know that colors can be a real deterrent if they aren't chosen carefully.

In the last few months, I've spent many hours on multiple listing sites and Craigslist looking at hundreds, if not thousands, of interior photos of houses, to find my next home. Here are a few of the things I've noticed:

- If the photos show a wall painted fire-engine red, I may not stick around to see anything else unless some architectural feature is so remarkable that it overpowers my negative feelings about the red wall.

- Bright blue doesn't do anything for me, either, not because of any emotional impact it has, but just because I don't own any furniture that looks good in a bright blue room. For that reason, I'd stay away from any of the primary, Crayola colors, unless it's in a child's bedroom.

- If a house looks like it's been "staged," I start looking very carefully at the photos to see what the sellers are trying to cover up.

I would still buy a house with a red living room, if everything else worked for me—I don't forget where the paint store happens to be, just because I'm in the market for a house, after all—but a photo of a red living room might keep me from getting excited enough about the house to call up and make an appointment to see it. For that reason, it seems wise to approach the subject of color with a reasonable amount of caution.

One thing that probably matters a lot is whether or not the paint is fresh and new, instead of scuffed up and tawdry. A new coat of paint really doesn't cost all that much, and it can help people feel better about the house when they first walk in the door. Some people even say that the new-paint smell can help sell a house, but I'm not sure if that's true or not.

Major projects—are they worth the trouble and expense?

Since I enjoy the creative process of moving walls around and installing new flooring, most of the major work of "getting the house ready" was done long before I decided that I needed to sell. However, there were some things that I probably should have done to get top dollar for my house. I listed those items on the "to do" list on my website, and I pointed them out to my buyer as she and her parents walked around the house.

If all of the repairs had been done *before* I posted my ad, it's possible that I could have added several thousand dollars to the price, but there's no way to know for sure.

During the housing boom, when I lived in Portland, Oregon, some friends of mine were watching the real estate market as closely as I was. The other couple and I all decided to sell our homes in 2006–just as national home prices started to fall, but a year before the market started to go down in Portland.

I had done a few remodeling jobs during the time I lived in my Portland house, and the projects probably helped the house sell much faster than it would have if I hadn't done the work–but once we made our decisions to sell it didn't me take long to get my house ready. I just repainted the interior walls, I cleaned out the clutter, and I hired an electrician to install a ceiling fan in the kitchen. (The fan went in because it was something I'd wanted to do ever since I moved in, and I couldn't bear to leave before it was done). I was ready to call a real estate agent just a few weeks after deciding to sell, and it sold two weeks later.

However, it took another *year* before my friends' house was ready to sell. Candace and John were working with an agent who recommended some major projects to make their house more appealing to buyers. They followed almost all of his suggestions, and even installed a new bathroom in the basement, at considerable expense. The only suggestion the agent made that they didn't follow was to dig up Candace's perennial flower beds. The agent thought the cottage garden would look like "too much work" to potential buyers, but the flowers stayed.

When their house did finally go on the market, it looked wonderful, and it sold quickly for the listing price. Fortunately (or I should say "luckily"), the extra year didn't hurt them, because home prices didn't begin to come down in earnest in the Portland area until 2007. However, during that year, they paid a spent a lot of money on the remodeling jobs, which they weren't able to do themselves; and they also paid an additional year's interest on their mortgage. Was the extra expense reflected in the price they got when the house finally sold? And did the extra bathroom and other remodeling projects help the house sell faster than it would have without them? There's no way to know.

We do know that it would have been a *very* expensive year if the local home prices had gone down in Portland in 2006, when the market started to slide in other areas of the country. If that had happened, the year's delay could have cost them some of the inflated equity in their home, and it could even have prevented them from finding a buyer at any price. Timing, as they say, is everything.

Since I decided to sell my house in La Grande specifically because I thought home prices would start to go down quickly, now that the banks were dumping their foreclosures at a steep discount, I didn't feel that I had any time to spare. Fortunately, my buyers didn't mind helping with the minor repairs that really should have been done before I posted my ad, and I was able to get moved before the 20% drop in home prices that happened in the last half of this year.

Clutter

The one thing that I am pretty sure about is that no matter what color the rooms are painted, they need to be clean and without excess clutter. I don't think that means that the house should look like a showroom—in fact, that's exactly what I *don't* want it to look like. However, people are embarrassed if they walk into a house with dirty laundry on the floor. I think people can imagine the house *without* the laundry, but it isn't what I want people to be thinking about when I'm trying to sell them my house.

People do need to walk comfortably through a room, and they shouldn't need to worry about tripping on the children's toys.

Cleaning out the clutter seems to be especially important in the garage. I know very few people who can actually use their garage for parking their car, because most of us fill our garages with all the stuff we own but rarely use. But still, most of us seem to believe that we *will* use our garage, either for the car or for a workshop.

Since my garage was full of stuff I really didn't need, I posted a lot of it on the local *FreeCycle.org* website, and some of it went to the Habitat for Humanity ReStore. If I had nicer stuff, I could have sold it on *Craigslist.org*.

Finding My Niche Market

W<small>HILE</small> I <small>DID</small> some sprucing up around the place to get it ready to sell, I was already starting to think about how I would write my ad on Craigslist.

Since I've been making a living online for many years, I'm in the habit of approaching all types of online sales from the point of view of *niche marketing*. That's the practice of writing ads and blog posts that appeal only to the small segment of the population that would actually be interested in the product, instead of trying to write a more generalized ad that might appeal to everyone. I use the idea of niche marketing when I create a website and when I write my blog posts. I imagine myself talking to a small group of people who are interested in a specific subject, like "sugar addiction," instead of trying to create a wide-open website about a huge subject, like "health." I understand sugar addicts very well, because I'm one of them.

I pay a lot of attention to the idea of niche marketing when I write my books, too. I recently wrote two popular books about paper mache crafts for non-professional artists who want to create great-looking sculptures and masks using inexpensive materials. In other words, they're popular with people like me. I don't try to create books about the general subject of sculpture, because then I wouldn't have a good mental image of the people I'm writing for., And I wouldn't know who to sell them to.

Since niche marketing works for me as a web publisher and author, I couldn't see why it wouldn't also work for selling a house online.

But to *make* it work, I needed to "see" the potential buyer who would be interested in my house, in the same way that I try to understand the people who are interested in my books and websites. And, if I was going to treat my buyers like the unique individuals that they were most likely to be, I would also need to look at my house to find out what made *it* unique, too. In other words, why did *I* like my house so much?

It's not always easy to see our own house from a buyer's point of view. When we live in a place for years, we might not even look at it all that much any more. It fits us, because we *made* it fit our interests and lifestyle–but what, exactly, did we do to make that happen? When I started searching for the special character of my house, I tried to see it as though I'd never been there before, the way a total stranger would see it. And that's not easy, because I knew every inch of the place.

Some real estate agents come at this from the opposite point of view–they try to see how a house could be changed to make it look more like houses you see in home magazines. They sometimes even recommend fairly expensive remodeling projects, not to make the house more comfortable for the people who currently live there, but to make it appeal to an imaginary "average" buyer.

That must work sometimes–agents *are* the experts in selling houses–but my way seems to work a lot better for me, and it costs a lot less money. I just decided that I'd use my ad and website to look for a buyer who would like my house, just as it was (after I spruced it up a bit with a few cans of paint and some de-cluttering, of course). If my theory was correct, I just had to figure out who my buyer might be, and then write my ad and website in a way that would appeal directly to them, and no one else.

As soon as I move in to a house, I start thinking about how I'll change it to make it more comfortable to live in. (In fact, I'm already in that planning stage for the house I'll move into next month). I think we all do this, although some people might say that I get a little more carried away when it comes to knocking down walls and digging up the lawn. Because we all change our houses to fit our own needs, houses tend to take on the character of the people who live in them, and that gave me some clues about the interests that my potential buyers might have. I would play up the character of the house, and write my ad and website so that only people who liked that character would be motivated to call me.

Looking at my house from a buyer's point of view

When I bought my house, it was a sound, well-built home in a good working-class neighborhood. A previous owner added plenty of insulation, new siding, new windows, and a new roof. The foundation was solid, and there was no rot. These were the features that helped me decide to buy my house in the first place, so I wrote them down on a list so I would be sure to include them in my Craigslist ad and website.

After I moved in, I made a few changes to the house that I thought almost anyone would appreciate. For instance, a previous owner turned the two-bedroom house into a one-bedroom house, by removing a wall between the living room and the front bedroom. I put the wall back in. I used the new second bedroom for my office, and for guests. I knew that most people prefer at least two bedrooms, even if they don't have kids.

I also improved the look of the bathroom by repairing the plaster wall, installing a new bathroom sink and new flooring, and painting the walls a nice dove-gray. And I replaced the living room carpeting with laminate flooring from Ikea.

Naturally, I would add the new flooring to my list of features to include in my ad, and people would see photos of the bathroom. All these small remodeling jobs were done while I lived in the house, for my own enjoyment– I don't make these changes because I'm some fancy-pants real estate investor or house flipper. I just happen to enjoy the creative process of making a house more comfortable. I also get a kick out of finding ways to make improvements without spending very much money.

The changes that I've already mentioned were nice, but they didn't really make the house stand out from the crowd. The things that actually mattered more to me from a niche marketing point of view were the changes that reflected my own unique personality and my interests. I like saving money, I'm concerned about the environment, I enjoy animals, and I'm a gardener who is concerned about food security.

These interests showed up in the large shelves I put up for my home-canned tomatoes, the shed that was turned into a greenhouse, the lawn that was dug up and turned into a very large vegetable garden that took up at least ¼ of the lot, the large number of fruit trees I planted, and the chicken run that I built under the grape arbor. I also turned a goldfish pond into a natural habitat for local frogs and native plants, and I put up several bird feeders.

All these things went on my list, so I could begin thinking about how I would write my ad for the people in town who had interests that were similar enough to mine so that they would see the oversized garden, the chicken house, the pond, and all the other changes as beneficial features, just like I did. This wasn't just helpful from a niche marketing point of view—it also meant that I didn't have to spend any money or time "fixing" the house, (by replanting the lawn, for instance), to meet the needs of a mythical "average" buyer. The list continued to grow as I spruced up the house and made it ready for it's new owner.

Setting a Price

ONCE ALL THE clean-up projects were done and the living room and kitchen had been painted, I was almost ready to start taking photos and writing my ads. I already had a list of features that made my house different from all the other houses on the market, and I had a good mental picture of the kind of person who would like to live in a house like mine—but I couldn't post an ad or build my website until I knew how much money I would be asking for my house.

I'm still not entirely sure that I chose the "right" price, but I'm not sure anyone *can* know, even if they have a good real estate agent helping them. That was especially true when I put my house on Craigslist, because of the sudden volatility of the local real estate market. After all, banks were suddenly dumping their foreclosures. Even if I hurried, any potential buyers would *also* know about those foreclosures, and they might expect a bargain. I needed a price that would make both of us happy, so I could get a fast sale without giving away my house.

Nationwide, housing prices have gone down 33.8% since I purchased my home back in 2006. That's a national average, though. As I mentioned earlier, listing prices in my city stayed about the same for about five years after the housing bubble burst. I thought that was about to change, though, and it turns out I was right. According to Zillow.com, home prices in La Grande, Oregon did finally start to go down just as I decided to sell, with the average listing price dropping a whopping 20.6% in the last half of 2012.

In other places, though, home prices seemed to be going back up, and some respected national experts (but not all) were starting to declare that the housing slump was over. It was still too soon to tell if the rising prices signified a long-term trend, or if it was a new bubble fueled by cash purchases by investors and a new spate of high-risk FHA mortgages—but no matter what might be causing prices to be coming up in *other* cities, they certainly seemed about ready to go down fast, in mine.

When prices are on a roller-coaster, and so many "experts" are contradicting each other with their predictions about future prices, it's especially tricky finding the true current value for a house, and once you choose a price, you'd almost need a crystal ball to know for sure you got it right.

Many of the local houses that were similar to mine were listed for $7,000 to $20,000 more than their owners paid for them during the housing bubble, but those houses sat on the market for months. Banks were starting to list their foreclosures for $15,000 to $40,000 less than their previous sales prices, and those were the houses that were selling. The wide disparity in listing prices made it difficult to know for sure how much I could expect to get for my house.

Online research

I went out to Zillow.com and I found several houses that were similar to mine that had sold within the last few years. I then compared those sold prices with the prices of currently listed homes on the local real estate websites, and paid a lot of attention to the amount of time each currently listed house had been on the market. Then I looked at how much the owners of listed houses paid for them, and how long they owned them. This way, I got a good feel for how much people would really pay for a house relative to it's previous value at the top of the real estate bubble, which is when most of the listed houses (and mine) were last purchased.

Offline research

Although I did get most of the important information off the Internet, I also walked by my "competition" to get a feel for the condition of the houses. This is something you can't always see in real estate listing photos. I knew my buyers were likely to have seen all the other houses currently for sale, so I wanted to know how my house would compare to them.

Why other listing prices don't help much

Many people try to determine the current value of their homes just by looking at comparable listings that they find on real estate sites. This doesn't help much, though, because it only tells you how much the owners of those houses *hope* someone will pay for them. This may be one reason why FSBOs have a reputation for being overpriced.

When I checked the current listings, I saw many homes priced much higher than the owners paid for them back at the top of the housing bubble. I even found a few that were listed at *more than double* their previous sales price (perhaps because the owners took out home equity loans that they need to pay off). Considering the economy, this doesn't seem entirely reasonable from a buyer's point of view, and that helps explain why these overpriced homes sat on the market for so long.

It's the actual sales that really matter

The listings I paid the most attention to were the ones for houses in my neighborhood that changed hands within the last year or two. When buyers work with a real estate agent, they're given this information when they try to determine the amount they'll offer on a house. This information is also available on the Internet where buyers can easily find it, even if they don't have an agent to help them. (The recent sales data will also be used by an appraiser when he determines the value of a house for a mortgage company.)

You can find this information for some (but not all) of the houses that have recently sold by going to Zillow.com. Do a search for your city, and then click on the "Filter" button. It's usually near the top of the page, but it seems to move around so you might have to hunt for it. On the drop-down box, click on "Recently Sold." If there are also a lot of houses currently for sale, you might want to un-click some of the other options, so the resulting map will be less crowded.

You can also get this information about a specific house by typing the address into Zillow.com. They don't include the price history of every house, but they do pull this information from public records, and any home that has sold within the last few years is likely to have this information on their site.

I knew buyers could see how much I paid for my house in 2006, and they would know that home prices had certainly not gone up in the years since. They could see how long other similar houses were sitting on the market, so they'd be able to guess that those other houses were overpriced. Unfortunately, they would also know, just as I did, that banks were starting to dump their foreclosures for prices that were much lower than the previous owners had paid a few years earlier, and those foreclosures were bound to influence a buyers when they made an offer.

I wanted a selling price for my own home that was low enough so I didn't scare away my buyers, but high enough so I would be happy after the sale was completed and I got my check. The fact that I didn't have a mortgage to worry about allowed me to be more flexible with the price than most people can, and I consider myself extremely lucky in that regard.

The price I finally chose was a few thousand dollars more than the price I paid for it in 2006. If the house had still only had one bedroom, like it did when I bought it, I probably would have priced it lower. Some people have suggested that I priced the house too low because it sold so fast, but I personally think I priced it exactly right.

Overpriced houses don't sell

When buyers look at a house that the sellers purchased just a few years ago, that previous sale price is often the most accurate information they can get when determining the value of the house. That wasn't true during the housing bubble, of course, but in normal times, house prices rise slowly, at the general rate of inflation. Most people are reluctant to offer more than they really think a house is worth, even if they really like it, because they worry about losing money later when it's time to sell.

When I was looking for my next home here in South Dakota, I fell in love with a house that had every feature that I wanted. The current owner bought the house three years ago and now wanted to turn around and sell it. The house had been completely remodeled, but this work was done before the current owner bought it (it said so right in the listing). The owner now wanted 15% more than she paid for it just three years earlier.

People almost always lose money if they sell a house so quickly, because they pay closing costs when they buy, and they pay a real estate commission when they sell. This house was priced high enough for the owner to recoup all of those costs, plus the owner's original down payment. From the standpoint of the seller, the listing price probably seemed entirely reasonable.

But as a buyer, I couldn't justify that 15% increase. I made an offer for the amount she previously paid for the house, as my own real estate agent suggested, and she rejected it. Her own agent allowed the offer to die without a response, so I had to walk away from the deal and find another house. It is now several months later, and the house has still not sold.

It's OK to ask for help

Since finding the right price is so difficult, some FSBO sellers turn to a good real estate agent. If you're honest with an agent and tell her you're thinking about selling the house yourself, they're usually happy to give you a few minutes of their time. You can call more than one agent, in fact, and interview them all. You can look at the "comps" they bring with them, and you can ask them how long the current listings have been on the market. You can also ask the agents how long they think it would take to sell your house at the price they suggest.

Even if you don't list the house with an agent right away, you'll then have some numbers you can call if you later decide that you aren't comfortable selling the house yourself, and you'd like some professional help.

It's important to remember, though, that most of the overpriced houses on the market have been listed by agents.

Some agents even deliberately suggest an initial listing price that they know is unreasonably high in order to get the listing, and then suggest lowering it a few months later because no buyers are looking at the house.

Did I choose the right price?

Looking back on the experience now, I think I did a rather good job of choosing my price. Once I made my decision, I then created an online marketing plan that would put my house directly in front of someone who would not only like the particular house I was selling, but who would recognize a good price when she saw it—and that meant I was able to sell *before* the impending 20.6% drop in home prices in my local market.

Photos

SINCE I'VE BEEN looking at a lot of Craigslist ads lately as a potential buyer, I am absolutely convinced that you *must* put photos in the ad. If *you* aren't convinced, play "buyer" for a few days, surf the real estate listings and Craigslist ads in your town, and take a note of which ads make you interested in the house. Also, be sure to pay attention to the ones that don't seem interesting at all.

For me, it's all about the photos, so I took lots. The Internet is, after all, a visual medium, and people expect to see images online.

Now that I've been looking at ads as a buyer, I'm even more convinced that the images are important. We all have a picture in our minds of what "home" looks like, even if we aren't completely conscious of it. I became very aware of this when I recently made an offer on a house that looks very much like the house I just sold. The most obvious feature of both houses is an enclosed south-facing porch.

Before I made my offer, I didn't realize that the porch was so important to me, and I didn't include "south-facing porch" on the list of "must-have" features that I gave to my real estate agent—but I knew I was going to buy that house as soon as I saw the photo of that porch in the online listing.

I took way more photos than I could fit into a Craigslist ad, so I built a simple WordPress website to hold them all. I'll show you how that was done in a later chapter.

I'm not a professional photographer, and my photos aren't all that great. However, all the hours that I spend surfing real estate sites and Craigslist ads has made me somewhat opinionated about the kinds of photos that help sell a house online, and the kinds of photos that can actually stop people from wanting to ever set foot in the place. I don't have any research to back up my opinions, but some of this just feels like common sense.

Lighting

Photos should always be taken in good light. If the day isn't bright enough and turning on all the lights doesn't help, I would go out and rent some more lights just for the photos. Nothing is more off-putting than a dark, dismal photo of a room. (I've seen online listings where every photo of every room in the house is dark, and it's kind of creepy.)

Take lots of photos

When I see a listing that has no interior photos at all, I assume there's something wrong with the inside of the house and I don't bother to call to make an appointment to see it. I think the ad should have as many photos as possible.

I admit that I haven't always followed my own advice about ignoring an ad with no photos. While I was waiting for my house to close, I briefly thought about moving to the Oregon coast. I found a listing online for an inexpensive house in a cute little town a few miles from the beach. I sent an email to the agent and asked her to send me interior photos (there weren't any in the listing), but she didn't respond.

Still, the price was great, so I made an appointment with a different agent, and drove across the state to see the house. As soon as I walked up to the front porch I could see why the agents didn't want to bother taking pictures–you could smell the mold without even going inside, and you could see the fake wood paneling peeling off the walls when you looked in the window.

I learned. If there are no pictures, I don't call.

No people in the photos

The photos should not include Uncle Harry sitting in the recliner drinking beer and watching the game on TV. There shouldn't be anyone *else* in the photos, either, even if they're cute.

No dogs?

A friend who looked at my photos told me I should retake them without the dog and cat. Her advice was probably good, but I ignored it, mostly because I'm lazy.

As it turned out, my buyers have a lovely dog, (a McNab cattle dog, as it turns out, the first one I've ever met), so seeing my critters in the pictures didn't bother them at all. This may actually be tied in with the idea of selling to a niche market– people who are allergic to dogs or cat hair probably shouldn't be looking at my house, anyway, so maybe there was no harm in leaving the pets in the photos. I certainly don't mind when I see a cat in a photo on someone else's Craigslist ad, but still–I'm on the fence about this one. I think my friend was probably right.

No clutter

I'm a natural slob, myself, but I know it's not all that hard to move the clutter out of the frame, even if you have to move it back again right after the photo is taken. (If you can't get a good photo without the clutter, it probably means that it's time to do some major reorganization anyway, to get the house ready to sell.) Owners have the advantage over real estate agents in this regard, because we can take photos over several days if we need to. Agents have to snap photos all at one time, and hope for the best.

My photos helped me see my house the way a stranger would. When I didn't like what I saw in a photo, I rearranged the furniture and got rid of a few more things, and then took the photo again.

The same friend who said "no dogs" also suggested removing the computer cord lying across the doorway to the kitchen, and the hoses lying on the lawn. I agreed with her (it really helps to get a second opinion from someone who isn't afraid to tell the truth). I cropped the hoses out of the outside photos, and then ordered a broadband router so I wouldn't need the long computer cord—but the house sold before I could take a new picture without it.

It is what it is

Some real estate agents try to make houses look better than they really are, or bigger than they really are (which isn't the same thing, in my opinion). Some agents even use a special lens that makes an average-sized living room look like the inside of a convention center. I think this is a mistake. As a buyer, I certainly don't appreciate spending time to go see a house that looks great in the agent's photos, only to discover that the agent carefully cropped out all the problems, like siding that needs new paint or a cracked and broken foundation.

In my opinion, the photos in an ad should be a good representation of what the buyers will see when they come look at the house in person.

Show both the inside and outside of the house

A lot of real estate listing photos show the inside of the house, but not the yard. That might work for a certain type of buyer, but as a gardener, I find it frustrating. (In some parts of the country, agents often forget to even mention the size of the lot!)

This was particularly important for the house I sold on Craigslist, because my yard was planted to fruit trees and corn and tomatoes. I took as many outside photos as I could, to appeal to potential gardeners (and to warn off people who are offended by anything other than a pristine lawn).

This, again, is marketing to a niche. People who are attracted to the words "easy-care lawn" would not want to buy my house. If I actually *did* have an easy-care lawn, I wouldn't just mention it—I'd be sure that potential buyers could see it in the ad.

As it turned out, my buyer never had a garden before, and she admits that she doesn't know the first thing about it. However, she has relatives who have already volunteered to help her, and she's quite excited to learn. The garden photos on my website helped pre-sell the house before she ever came to see it in person.

The same thing is true of the bright turquoise walls and warm white cabinets that showed up in the photos of the kitchen. The images helped me find a buyer through my

Craigslist ad who immediately fell in love with the place. Even more importantly, as far as I'm concerned, I didn't have to show my house to anyone who *wouldn't* like it, because I put lots of photos in my ad and on my website.

Saving images for the Web

Some photo-sharing sites have software that can automatically edit uploaded images to make them load faster, but Craigslist won't do this for you. Since very large photos slow down the load time of a web page, it's important to reduce the size of images before putting them online. Almost all digital cameras have the ability to save images with either high resolution, (which you would need if the photos were to be printed) or at a low resolution that gives you a relatively small size. A low resolution is perfect when you'll be posting the photos online.

Of course, every camera is different, so they have different controls for saving images at different resolutions. I happen to have a Canon PowerShot ELPH 300 HS. On my camera, I click the FUNC SET button on the back, and then scroll down the list shown in the display window until I reach the big "L."

Then I scroll down again to click on the big "S," which will give me an image 640 x 480 pixels, the smallest size my camera will save. The message in the window shows that this is the correct control to choose when sending a photo as an email attachment. It's also the perfect setting for images posted on Craigslist.

Other cameras will have controls in different places, but they almost always have a setting for low-resolution images. If you aren't sure how to find the settings, there should be a manual that came with your camera or image editing software.

The Website

BEFORE I POSTED my ad on Craigslist, I put together a very simple website. I have never seen any other ad on Craigslist with a link to a separate website, except for ads that are posted by professional real estate agents. When you think about it, just the fact that I included a link to my website made my ad stand out.

I know that most people who pick up a book about selling a house on Craigslist will not be expecting a chapter or two about building websites. After all, posting an ad sounds easy, and most people think that building a website is hard. Besides, nobody *else* does it, so what's the point?

Of course, the fact that nobody else does it *is* the point. I wanted my ad to stand out from all the other ads on the Craislsist.org website. I personally believe the website was one of the reasons why my online marketing campaign was so successful, and I would build another one if I ever sold another house–even if I sold the house through an agent.

It probably also seems a bit backwards to be talking about the website first, when a buyer will only see the website *after* they see the Craigslist ad. I dithered over the placement of this chapter for just that reason, but as a seller, I had to build the website *before* I posted my ad. Since I'm telling you the story about how I sold my house in six days, I need to show you the entire process, in the proper order.

If all I wanted to do was show more pictures than Craigslist will allow, I could have used a Flickr account or some other photo-sharing site. However, I wanted much more than that—I wanted people who found my ad on Craigslist to have access to at least as much information as they would find on a real estate agent's website. In fact, since I was *competing* with those professional agents, I wanted to give buyers even more information than agents usually put in their online listings—and there just isn't room for all the information I wanted to include on a standard Craigslist ad.

Another good reason to build a website is the way that ads are formatted on the Craigslist site. All of the descriptive text that you type into their online form will appear at the top of the post. Any photos you add come *after* all of the text. If I added all the information that I thought was needed in order to encourage a buyer to call me, all the photos of my house would end up way down at the very bottom of the page, after a long column of text. The Internet is a visual medium, and I wanted the photos in my ad to be seen right at the top, without needing to scroll.

By using the website for all the extra information that most people leave out of their ads, and for all the extra photos that Craigslist doesn't have room for, I got the best use of the Internet for selling my house.

The one group of people who do regularly link to a website inside their Craigslist ads are real estate agents. Unfortunately, most agents kind of skip the ad portion, and just use Craigslist as a place to put a link to the listing on their own website. I think this is a mistake, too. I've been selling things online for a lot of years, and I know that every time you ask a reader to do *anything,* even as small a thing as clicking on a link, you need to give them a very good reason to do it. You have to "sell" the click—and that's what many agents forget to do.

So, there were really two important parts of my online marketing:

1. My **Craigslist ad** gave me the opportunity to sell visitors on the idea of visiting my website.

2. **The website** was used to sell visitors on the idea of picking up the phone and calling me.

Both the ad and the website also helped weed out all the home buyers that I didn't want to talk to at all—the ones who were looking for a different kind of house than the one I had to sell.

You can take a look at the website I made at *LaGrandeHouse.com.* I also added a photo of the site at the end of this chapter, so you can see how basic it looks. It was built using WordPress, which is free.

When you visit the site you won't see it exactly the same way people did when my house was still on the market. I removed the address of the house to protect my buyer's privacy, and I removed my phone number (since I moved out of state, and the old number won't work now anyway.) I added a small ad to direct readers to this book on Amazon.com, just in case someone accidentally stumbles onto my site when they do a Google search; and I added one extra page so you could see what the expired Craigslist ad looked like when it was still online (there's a link to it in the sidebar). That sounds like a lot of changes, but it's not, really—everything else is exactly the way it looked during that six days when my house was still for sale.

Since I know that many people will still be skeptical, here are a few more reasons why I thought the website was important:

- **You control the look**

You can make a website look exactly the way you want it to. Craigslist is great, but they do limit your options, like only allowing 8 photos. To make my website stand out, I added a nice photo of my house at the top, which was taken through the branches of one of the trees on the parking strip, and I chose a background color of the site that looked nice with the header photo.

These things are very easy to do, and they make the site look completely different from a standard page on Craigslist. Then I added tons of photos.

I do want to mention, though, that I wouldn't spend a whole lot of time designing a snazzy website—I was trying to sell a house, not my design services. A simple, basic website is all I needed, so that's what I built.

- **You can add as much info as you want**

Most people rely entirely on a short description of their house in a paragraph on Craigslist, and perhaps a few photos. Some sellers don't even bother telling you how much money they want for their house or what town it's located in, which means you have to call them to find out. In contrast, my website has much more information than I could possibly fit onto a Craigslist ad, and it was written specifically to encourage a potential buyer to call me and make an appointment to see the house. I'll go through all the information that I included, and why I thought it was important, a bit later in this chapter.

- **No limit on how long your site stays online**

Your website will stay up until *you* choose to take it down (Craigslist ads expire after a set amount of time).

- **Easy web address for print ads and signs**

You can buy a domain name that is easier to include in a print ad for about $15, or you can use a free WordPress or Blogger-hosted site with a name that's only slightly longer. In contrast, a Craigslist URL (web address), is really long and difficult to type. If you do any advertising offline, this really matters. This is what a Craigslist web address looks like:

http://siouxfalls.craigslist.org/reo/3453464652.html

And this is what *my* web address looks like:

http://LaGrandeHouse.com

Try to imagine which one would be easier to type into a browser if you were seeing them printed in a little classified ad in the local paper.

To show you why this is important, I'll give you a real example. One day when I was walking my dog I saw a new "for sale by owner" sign in front of a neighbor's house. The sellers added a note to the sign telling people to "get more information on Craigslist." When I got home I sat down at my computer and searched for their ad. It took a long time to find it. Since the address of the house wasn't shown in the title, I had to open up every ad for every FSBO house in town, and then look at the photos to see if I recognized the house. Not only did the sellers waste my time, but they also encouraged me to look at every other competing ad on Craigslist!

It would have been so much better if they'd written "go to MyHouse.com for more info," instead. But, of course, they *couldn't* do that, because they didn't build their own website.

- **The link can be posted on other sites**

If you want your house to appear for sale on Zillow.com, (their listings are free), you can include a link to your website. You can also put a link to your site when you comment on blogs and forums, and you can add it to the description area if you decide to put a video of your house on YouTube. Or you can send the link in an email to all your friends, just in case they know someone looking for a house.

Web site basics:

I'll go into the details of building a WordPress website in a later chapter, (it's easy) but these are the basic bits of information that I thought a potential buyer would want to see:

- The **price,** shown in bold at the top of the page. (I won't call if an ad doesn't include the price, and I think that's true for a lot of other people, too.)

- The **address** of the house, in case people wanted to drive by to check out the neighborhood before calling. (If I lived in a high-crime area, I'd probably leave off the address.)

- Lots of **pictures**, of both the **inside** and **outside** of the house, on two separate pages.

- A long bullet-list of **features**. This is the list that I started writing when I was getting the house ready for sale. Putting these items on a list is easier than writing a paragraph that tries to include them all, and the list format is easier to read quickly—which is important when you're trying to catch the attention of people online. I made separate lists for the inside and outside of the house, because the photos for them were also on different pages.

- A short paragraph with a **description** of the house, without any of the usual real-estate hype, and written especially for a person who might like all the same things about the house that I do.

- **Contact information** at the bottom of every page, and on the sidebar of every page.

- A **to-do list**. This is the equivalent of the disclosure form that is required when you list a house with an agent. I learned, back when I sold real estate professionally for a few months, that the more honest you are about possible defects in the house, the more willing buyers are to accept them. I wanted no surprises–especially since I intended to tell anyone who saw the house that any repairs would have to be done *and paid for* by the buyers–I was selling the house as-is.

- A **market research** page. To create this page, I went out to one of the local real estate websites and found a few houses that were similar to mine, and in a similar price range. I also went out to Zillow.com to find a few houses that had recently sold in my neighborhood. I felt that adding this information reinforced the feeling that I was being professional about the whole process, and that I was being realistic about the current value of my house.

- A **contact page**. Even though my phone number was listed twice on every page, a lot of people look for a link to a contact page when they visit a site. I wanted to make it as easy as possible for people to call me.

- **Links** to every page on the site from every other page. Since this is a WordPress site, the links are all added automatically.

When you use WordPress or one of the other free blogging platforms, a website can be completed in just a few days, even if you've never built a website before.

I actually built a similar website when I sold my tiny house six years ago in Portland, Oregon, even though I listed that house with a real estate agent. Instead of my own contact information, I posted the phone number of my real estate agent. I also put an ad on the Portland Craigslist, with a link to my site. A WordPress site doesn't take much time, so I think it's well worth the effort—especially since hardly anyone else bothers to do it. It never hurts to stand out from the crowd.

Website details

I've just gone over the basic items that went into the site, but now I'd like to go through them in detail so you can see how I used the idea of *niche marketing* when I wrote the lists and description. Every house is unique, and I wanted to make sure that anyone reading my website would see the features that set my house apart from the other houses on the market. Remember, I wanted the ad and website to appeal to the kind of person who would really like living in my house, and I wanted to *warn off* any potential lookie-loos who would hate it. (After all, what's the point of showing a house to someone who wouldn't want to buy it, anyway?)

Here's the list of features that I placed below the photos on the home page:

- **Features:**

- 2 Bedrooms, 1 Bath
- Sq ft: 864
- Detached Garage with Alley Access
- Big and Bright Eat-In Kitchen with Vintage Colors and Tons of Storage
- Partial Basement
- Natural Gas Furnace and Water Heater
- Appliances Stay, Including Refrigerator, Washer, Dryer, and Gas Cook Stove
- Lot: 60 x 110, Fenced, with Fruit Trees and Large Garden Area
- Year built: 1915
- 9 foot ceilings
- Ceiling fan in living room
- Newer laminate flooring in the living room and front bedroom
- All windows are double-pane vinyl
- Covered back deck
- Small pond with water plants; a favorite spot for frogs and visiting birds
- Good neighborhood, close to Greenwood school

This list includes more information than you find on many professional real estate listings. The bullet-pointed list is easy to read, and it gives readers the information quickly, without wasting their time.

- **Links**

Directly below the list are two links, one to the page where they'll see photos of the yard and garden, and another link to the page on Zillow.com where the readers can see the sales history of the house. Since the information is important to a buyer and it's publicly available, I thought it was only nice to make it easy for them to find.

- **Description**

Below the links I placed a short paragraph, which is similar to the descriptions that are written by real estate agents. However, I tried to avoid the usual real estate hype that makes a reader translate all the words ("cozy" means cramped, etc.). The descriptive paragraph is shown below:

. . .

There's nothing fancy about this house, but it's comfortable. The smaller size and plenty of insulation keeps heating costs down in the winter. Most of the lot has been switched over from grass to garden, and there's plenty of storage inside for your harvest of veggies and fruit - and eggs, too, if you want. You can even get a head start on your garden by starting seeds in the big greenhouse window on the enclosed front porch."

. . .

I used this same paragraph on my Craigslist ad. I start out in a somewhat humble manner, just to make sure readers know I'm not trying to make the house sound any more wonderful than it is. Most people seem to find this refreshing, because we've all read the many real estate ads that all seem to advertise the same "perfect" house.

Most of this information was already shown in the list of features, but the paragraph form allowed me to present the information again in a new way. I wanted readers to imagine themselves in a house like this, so they could feel for themselves if it was a good fit for them or not.

The paragraph also points out the features that I particularly valued, in hopes that it would speak to my "niche market." For instance, the insulation will appeal to a budget-minded buyer, because it says the house is going to be warm in the winter without costing an arm and a leg. It also says the size of the house is a benefit rather than a drawback. Some people would agree with this, and some people won't. I only wanted to show the house to the people who like small houses.

I spent most of the paragraph on the garden, because that's the first thing they'll see when they drive up to the house—I wanted no surprises. They also needed to know that chickens have been in residence in the recent past (and that they could live there in the future, too, if the buyer was interested). I think it's obvious that "average" buyers would *not* be impressed by this description. I wasn't trying to reach an average buyer, because I didn't have an average house.

- **Yard and Garden Page**

Again, the paragraph at the top of the yard and garden page emphasizes that this is *not* a house with a well-manicured lawn and easy-care shrubs. There's also an honest description of the current condition of the garden, which was not at its best.

If the house and yard *had* been perfect, I probably would have concocted some imaginary defect to be humble about—I've found that an admission that a house *isn't* perfect actually increases the chance that a person reading the ad will end up buying the house, but I can't explain why. Perhaps it's just because it's not what a buyer expects to see in an ad. However, this is another one of those things that seems to go counter to the general wisdom of real estate professionals, and it could just be that I've been remarkably lucky.

Here's the description that appeared above the photos on my yard and garden page:

. . .

For the last six years, the yard has been used as an organic urban mini-farm. The yard is a bit overgrown at the moment – I've been very busy lately with my artwork and blog. A few hours of pleasant outside work would get it in shape quickly. (A bit more sun would help, too!) The garden looked a lot better last year, and it will look better again, I'm sure.

I gave the chickens away this spring because I went on a no-egg diet, but if you want chickens or ducks, the space is all set up for them. Or you could use the space for an indoor-outdoor dog run, or storage.

See a list of fruit trees below the photo gallery.

. . .

I was trying for a conversational tone that didn't feel too much like I was trying hard to sell anything. I did intend to post a video I took in a previous year when the garden looked much better, but the house sold before I got around to it.

There are nine photos below the text, showing the yard, the garden, the greenhouse, and the outside of the house. There is also a photo of the small pond. As promised, I included a list of fruit trees and bushes below the photos.

- **To-Do list**

Nobody ever puts a list of defects on a Craigslist ad. I wouldn't put a list like this on a Craigslist ad either, because it would take up too much room, but I had plenty of extra space on my website. I really did want people to know the house wasn't perfect (every house this age has some problems, and there's no harm in admitting the obvious).

When potential buyers find the defects on their own, I've noticed that the problems seem to take on more importance. I've never done a scientific study or anything, but in my experience it really does seem to help smooth the way to successful negotiations later on if you get everything out in the open right from the start. This list appeared on a separate page, which said the following:

. . .

There are several things that should be done to the house that I haven't gotten around to doing yet:

- *Replace ceiling light fixture in laundry area*

- *Replace several treads on stairs to basement*

- *Paint outside trim*

- *Install drip edge on gutter along roof over back deck.*

- *Some of the floor boards on front porch need to be replaced*

- *Replace cracked outdoor water hydrant*

This may not be a complete list – buyers are responsible for getting a professional inspection before closing.

. . .

I really did include every problem that I could think of, but the appraiser found more problems, of course—they always do). To my surprise, the inspector and appraiser left off many of the items that I included, and those items were not fixed before the house closed. I'm sure the new buyers already have a new list of things they want to fix or change.

You can see the main page of the website on the following pages, or see it in color at:

http://LaGrandeHouse.com

LA GRANDE HOME FOR SALE | YARD AND GARDEN PHOTOS | MARKET RESEARCH | CONTACT

La Grande House for Sale by Owner

$77,650
La Grande, OR 97850

Details below photo gallery. (Click on Photo to see Full-Sized Image)

Contact info originally appeared here.

Top half of home page, "above the fold."

Features:

- 2 Bedrooms, 1 Bath
- Sq ft: 864
- Detached Garage with Alley Access
- Big and Bright Eat-In Kitchen with Vintage Colors and Tons of Storage
- Partial Basement
- Natural Gas Furnace and Water Heater
- Appliances Stay, Including Refrigerator, Washer, Dryer, and Gas Cook Stove
- Lot: 60 x 110, Fenced, with Fruit Trees and Large Garden Area
- Year built: 1915
- 9 foot ceilings
- Ceiling fan in living room
- Newer laminate flooring in the living room and front bedroom
- All windows are double-pane vinyl
- Covered back deck
- Small pond with water plants; a favorite spot for frogs and visiting birds
- Good neighborhood, close to Greenwood school

Click here for photos of yard and garden.
Click here for house values and sales history shown on Zillow.com.

There's nothing fancy about this house, but it's comfortable. The smaller size and plenty of insulation keeps heating costs down in the winter. Most of the lot has been switched over from grass to garden, and there's plenty of storage inside for your harvest of veggies and fruit – and eggs, too, if you want. You can even get a head start on your garden by starting seeds in the big greenhouse window on the enclosed front porch.

If you would like to see the house, please call the owner at 555-000-0000

Bottom half of home page.

The Craigslist Ad

Now THAT MY website was built, I needed to make sure that a potential buyer could find it. The easiest way for me to do that was to put an ad on Craigslist. The ad would have a link to the website, and just enough information about the house to make people click on the link.

Most people already know about Craigslist, so they automatically go to that site when they're trying to find a house to buy directly from an owner. However, since there might be a few people in town who *didn't* know about Craigslist, I also sent in an ad to the local want-ad paper. The paper was printed once a week and I missed the deadline, so the print ad didn't appear until after the house was already sold.

If the house had *not* sold so quickly, I also would have added it on the local Zillow.com site, to make sure my house would be seen if a buyer searched that site for local listings; and I probably would have put a simple video on YouTube, with a link to my site in the description. I didn't get a chance to try either of those things, though, because my house sold so fast.

Making a Craigslist ad stand out

The most important thing I had to consider when posting my ad was to make sure people could actually find it among all the *other* ads on Craigslist. To show you an example of what a potential buyer will see when they arrive at their local Craigslist, I recently went out to the Craigslist.org site that covers SE South Dakota and I found the following ads at the top of the real estate page:

Home for sale in Sioux Falls, SD - $164900 / 3br - 2080ft² - (2 miles west of Tea Ellis Road Hyway 42) pic map owner

Check this out! Price Reduced! 3 bed 2 bath home! Make offer! - $136900 / 3br - (Sioux Falls SD 57110) img broker

Newer 4bd/2ba Ranch-style house w/new flooring & appliances - $169900 / 4br - 2160ft² - (Flandreau, SD) img map owner

Duplex rental investment property for sale - $72500 / 3br - 1200ft² - (Sioux Falls, SD) pic owner

*>*OPEN HOUSE Dec. 16th 1-2:30*>* - (Sioux Falls) img broker

Acreage 15 Minutes from Sioux Falls - $95000 / 1806ft² - (Worthing Area - Just off I-29) pic img broker

3.5 Acres 20 Minutes from Sioux Falls - 3br - 1357ft² - (SE South Dakota) pic img broker

Spacious Ranch Home - $114900 / 3br - 1236ft² - (Canton) pic broker

Spacious Home on Cul-de-Sac - $155000 / 5br - 2578ft² - (SW Sioux Falls) pic img broker

This is not a complete list—over 30 ads were posted on that day, and 8 days worth of ads were shown on the first page of the real estate section. Each ad is competing with every other ad for the attention of a limited number of potential buyers. It's the job of the person posting the ad to make sure their ad stands out from all the rest.

- **Writing a descriptive title**

Online, readers tend to scan a list quickly, so it's important to write a descriptive title that will let people know exactly what the ad is about. I think most of the titles on the list above are reasonably descriptive and well-written. The three that might need a bit of work are the first one, which doesn't really describe any of the unique features of the house; the second one, which seems to be advertising the seller's desperation instead of telling us about the house; and the one that just says "Open House," and the date, which gives us no useful information at all.

- **Working with the Craigslist search engine**

There are several hundred ads to look through on any given day, and most of them are for houses that won't interest a specific buyer. The newest ads are the only ones immediately visible, because older ads get pushed to the bottom of the page or onto another page entirely. And the main real estate page shows ads for houses in many different cities, because the local Craigslist sites almost always cover a wide portion of a state.

Buyers can save a lot of time by using the search feature on Craigslist. This tool will pull up a list of houses for sale in the right town, with the right price, the right number of bedrooms, etc. Fortunately, Craigslist is set up so that if you fill in all the blanks while you're posting your ad, it will be easy for your buyers to find it.

I paid a *lot* of attention to the items that show up right *after* the title—the price, square footage, number of bedrooms, and location. These are the things that matter most to the search engine built into the Craigslist site.

When you go to the real estate listings on any local Craigslist you'll see the "search for" box at the top of the page. You can type in a word, just like you can on Google, and Craigslist will look through all its ads for that specific word. If someone uses the term "lake house," for instance, any post that contains the words "lake house" would appear on the search results. You can also use the text search to find houses that are located in a specific town or city.

Below the text search tool, you can find tools that search for a price range and the specific number of bedrooms. In addition, you can choose how you want the search results to appear:

- You can choose only those ads that contain images;

- You can see your search results as a simple list, or;

- As a list with thumbnails of the first images that appear in the ads, or;

- In "map view," which shows exactly where all the houses are located on a map.

The Craigslist search engine finds the right ads by using the information you give it when you fill in a few text boxes on their ad posting form.

If you have a two-bedroom house but you leave out the number of bedrooms when you post your ad, your ad won't appear *at all* in the search results when someone does a search for a two bedroom house. If you leave out the location, as many people seem to do, the ad won't show up if someone chooses to search using the map view, and it won't show up on the list if someone does a text search for houses in your town. And if you don't put in any images at all, someone searching only for ads with images will never see it.

I obviously didn't want my ad to be invisible to readers who used the search feature on Craigslist, so I filled in all the blanks.

If you look at the ads on the list on page 67, you'll see that the only ad that *doesn't* include the price, bedrooms and square footage information is the "Open House" ad that was posted by a broker. Brokers have lots of houses to sell, so maybe they can afford to be this lazy. I only had *one* house to sell, so I spent a few seconds and filled in all the blanks.

Posting the ad on Craigslist.org

Once you know what you're going to put in an ad, posting it on Craigslist is pretty easy. The only tricky part is getting the images online, and that really isn't all that hard. This is how you get your ad on Craigslist.

- **Find your Local Craigslist**

Go to *Craigslist.org* and choose your city and state from the list.

- **Post to Classifieds**

Click on the "post to classifieds" link, which you'll find at the top on the left-hand column.

- **Type of Posting, and Category**

Choose the type of posting, which would be "housing offered." The next page asks you to choose a category, and you'll probably want to choose "real estate - by owner."

- **Price, Bedrooms, Square Feet, and Location**

Now you see those important text boxes that give you a place for listing the price, the number of bedrooms, the square feet of the house, the posting title, and the specific location. Remember, this information is used by the Craigslist search engine to help buyers find the ads they're looking for. You *can* leave these boxes blank, but if you do, your ad might not be seen by the one person who really wants to buy your house. I highly recommend filling in all the blanks. I certainly did, when I posted my own ad.

Even if you absolutely must leave some of these boxes blank (although I can't imagine why you would want to), I would *strongly* recommend including the price in every ad. People don't want to waste their time trying to find out if a house is within their price range. In fact, leaving it out feels almost disrespectful, because it says the seller expects a buyer to go to the extra trouble and call them to get information that almost every other ad includes as a matter of course. Many people simply won't bother. I know *I* don't call if a price is left off an ad, and I'm pretty sure I'm not the only who feels this way.

- **Posting Title**

The posting title is really important, because it can help the ad stand out in the list on the main real estate page. I think it should tell readers just enough to "sell" a potential buyer on the idea of clicking on the post title so they can read the rest of the ad.

When I sat down to write the title of my Craigslist ad, I chose to mention the most obvious features–the size of the house (small) and the size of the garden (big). This is what I came up with:

Small House, Large Garden in La Grande

This doesn't sound like a great sales pitch, I admit, but I wanted to weed out any potential buyers who were looking for a McMansion on a small, "easy-care" lot.

- **Email Address**

Below the title boxes on the Craigslist form, you'll find a box for your email address, and you can choose to "anonymize" it. (I've never seen this word anywhere but on Craigslist.) If you choose that option, readers can send you questions by email, but they won't be given your actual email address. There are a lot of spammers out there who find email addresses on Craigslist, so I definitely recommend choosing the "anonymize" option.

I've noticed that quite a few advertisers tell people they won't answer emails, and ask readers to call, instead. If you're worried about getting spam, or if you just don't like to check your inbox regularly, this is a good idea. Just make sure you actually put your phone number in the ad!

- **Posting Description**

In the Posting Description box, I used the same paragraph that I put on the bottom of my web page. I felt it was just enough to make someone curious. Then, just below the description, I asked readers to click on a link to my website to get more information and see more photos.

To make a link clickable on Craigslist, you need to include the entire URL (web address). Since I'm always worried about typing the address wrong, (and that would keep the link from working), I open up my website on my browser, and then copy the address that shows at the top of the browser window. Then I paste it into the ad. That way, you end up with all of it (including the http://) and there can't be any typos.

- **Location**

Below the Posting Description field, you see text boxes that allow you to give the street and cross street, city and zip code. This information is used for the map that is found right below your ad. Again, I can't imagine why anyone would choose to leave these areas blank, unless you're really worried about people who drive by to check out the house before they call. If you live alone, or if the house is empty and might be vandalized, I suppose it might be best not to include the address.

- **Add Images**

On the next page, you'll find a box that allows you to post up to 8 images on the ad. Click on the "Browse" button, go to the file where your images are located on your hard drive, choose one, and click the "open" button. You then have a chance to add seven more images.

If you didn't save the images with a low resolution, they may take a very long time to load. If that happens, you will want to go back to the image editing software that came with your camera and edit them so they're smaller. When you're finished adding photos, click on the "Done with Images" button. If you change your mind and don't want an image to show up on your ad, click on the little [x] below the photo.

I only used a few photos in my ad, but I added enough images so people would be able to tell if they would like the house or not. They also knew they could see more photos if they wanted to, by clicking the link to my website.

- **View Your Ad**

On the next page you can see exactly how your ad will appear to people who visit the Craigslist site. If you see anything that needs to be changed, you can do that now by clicking on any of the three edit buttons below the ad. If it looks OK, click the "Continue" button.

Check Your Email inbox

Craigslist will send you an automated email that has a subject line beginning with POST/EDIT/DELETE. You will need to click on the link in the email and agree with the terms of service before your ad is posted online. Since you may want to make changes in your ad later, or even delete it if your house sells right away, be sure to keep the email so you can go back and make changes as often as you like. On the next page, you can see how my ad looked on Craigslist. You can see it in color and full-size if you go to my website at:

http://LaGrandeHouse.com/craigslist-ad

$77650 / 2br - 864ft² - Small House, Large Garden in La Grande

Date: 2012-07-07, 9:20AM PDT
Reply to: *your anonymous craigslist address will appear here*

There's nothing fancy about this house, but it's comfortable, well-insulated, and easy to heat. There's a large, sunny eat-in kitchen with vintage colors and tons of storage. Most of the lot has been switched over from grass to garden, and there's a spot for your chickens or ducks - or use that area for an indoor outdoor dog run. Small pool off the covered deck is a favorite spot for frogs and birds. North La Grande location is an easy walk to downtown, and just a few blocks from Greenwood school.

See more photos and more complete description at http://LaGrandeHouse.com

If you would like to see the house, please call the owner at -- 541 ···

After My Ad Was Posted

Now THE WEBSITE was online, and the ad was posted on Craigslist. What happened next would not be duplicated with a different buyer, of course, because this process is so personal. I happened to get really lucky, because my buyer and her parents were wonderful team players. You just have to cross your fingers and hope you find a buyer who will work with you and keep you informed about any problems that might come up with their mortgage company. In other words, you hope for the best. Fortunately, the best is what I got.

The ad was posted on a Saturday, and I received a call from the buyer's father on Sunday. He made an appointment to come with his wife and daughter to see the house after he got off work on Monday.

The parents are helping their daughter buy the house, and they had already spent several months looking at houses in the area before I posted my ad. That meant they were very familiar with the limited number of houses available in my price range.

Many of the houses they looked at needed major repairs, especially the bank-owned houses in foreclosure. Because they'd done their research, they could tell from the description and photos on my ad and website that the price I'd chosen was fair. They may even have thought they were getting an exceptionally good deal—and that's exactly what I was hoping for. I wanted to sell fast so I could move before prices started to drop, and before winter weather arrived.

My buyers liked what they saw when they looked at the photos and read through the descriptions and feature lists on my website, so they knew a lot about the house even before they called.

- **The buyers saw the house**

On that Monday afternoon, the buyer and her parents arrived at the house right on time. They brought their dog along, so I invited her in, too–I had a dog-friendly house, and it didn't make sense to leave her outside in the car. This is just one more thing that made this experience more personal than it would have been if the buyers were looking through the house with an agent.

The buyers had already seen the photos on the Craigslist ad and on the website, and they had been drawn in by the photos of the yard and by the colors, especially the turquoise kitchen. Some real estate agents might have suggested installing new cabinets and appliances before even listing the house, in order to appeal to their imaginary "average" buyers. Instead, I played up the country-kitchen feel with the turquoise walls and warm white paint on the cabinets, and hoped that a potential buyer would enjoy the old-fashioned kitchen as much as I did. And it worked.

The buyers had already seen my list of things that needed to be fixed, because it was posted on my website. The inspections hadn't been done yet, of course, so I couldn't guarantee that I knew everything that was wrong with the house, but I did put down everything I knew about at the time. That meant that the buyers knew about potential problems before they came to see the house, so they obviously weren't put off by it.

While we walked around the yard, I pointed out the peeling paint up high in the eaves, and I mentioned that I couldn't afford to make any major repairs. My buyers would need to fix anything that was required by their mortgage lender.

Since the buyers had been looking at houses for several months, I think it was a relief for them to find an affordable house that only needed minor repairs. They told me they looked at one foreclosure that had plumbing fixtures ripped out of the walls–my peeling eaves were minor, compared to that. They also knew that they could back out of any deal if their inspector found problems that would be too expensive.

- **Purchase agreement signed**

The next step was to get a standard purchase offer form, and fill it out. The buyers went to the local escrow company, which sells the forms for a small fee. They came back on Friday and we filled out the form together. The buyer then took the form to a local real estate attorney, just to make sure we'd done it right. This cost them about $50, but it gave the buyers some peace of mind.

- **The escrow company**

The buyers gave me a check for the earnest money, and I took this check, along with a copy of the completed form, to the escrow company. They hold the check in their escrow account, and they apply the funds towards the buyers' down payment at closing. It only took a few minutes for the lady at the escrow company to set up a new file for us, and get the process started.

- **The mortgage**

The buyers had been pre-approved by a mortgage company, so their next step was to take their copies of the form to their loan officer, and get the process started there.

- **The inspection**

The buyers hired an inspector to carefully look over the house and find anything that was in disrepair. In his opinion, only a few things would need to be fixed immediately to satisfy FHA. Unfortunately, the inspector did not look at the garage, and that brought us some grief a bit later in the process. That was not his fault though–the buyers didn't think the bank would care about the shape of the old garage at the back of the lot, so they didn't ask him to inspect it.

Fortunately, their inspector was quite pleased with how solid the house is, considering its age. His positive opinion helped to stave off any potential buyer's remorse.

- **The repairs, stage 1**

The buyer's parents showed up at the house the next weekend with a gallon of paint for the eaves, and some lumber to replace a piece of wood that had become water damaged because a previous owner installed the roof over the deck incorrectly. I painted all of the trim around the windows, because it was easy to reach them from a six-foot step ladder. The buyer's mother painted the eaves on the south side of the house, which was the only area where the paint was noticeably peeling. Her husband replaced the board on the deck's roof. (The daughter, who was actually buying the house, had to attend a conference out of town that weekend, so she couldn't help).

All of the repairs the inspector suggested were finished by Sunday afternoon. That weekend while we worked and talked, we discovered that my buyer's grandfather, who once owned a dude ranch, had been a good friend of my great uncle, who owned a gold mine on the same mountain. In fact, our two families may even be distantly related. My buyer's father kept us entertained with some great stories about the two old characters, which kept us laughing as we worked.

- **The title report**

In the meantime, the mortgage company sent their paperwork to the title and escrow company, and a title report was created. A copy of the report was sent to us. As soon as he saw it, the buyer's father called me in something of a panic–the title company mistakenly used the records of someone with his first and last name (but a different social security number) and the initial title report listed three pages of liens against this other person for unpaid child support. Since it was an obvious error, a few phone calls were made and the error was corrected.

- **The appraisal**

Next, the FHA appraisal was scheduled. The buyers came to the house at the same time and we all had a chance to talk to the appraiser and find out if any more repairs were needed. He told us that some peeling paint on the garage door was the only thing that had to be fixed in order for the house to qualify for an FHA loan.

- **The repairs, stage 2**

I scraped and painted the garage door that Friday, and the appraiser drove by again to make sure it had been done.

At this point, we assumed that we just needed to wait for the appraiser to finish writing his report. When it was received by the mortgage company, the loan papers would go to the underwriters for final approval.

Things never go that smoothly, though. For no obvious reason, the appraiser discovered, perhaps when looking at the photos that would go with his report, that the garage roof needed to be replaced. This, of course, was *after* he'd already been to the house twice already, so it came as a bit of a shock. However, it still needed to be done, or the bank wouldn't make the loan.

- **The repairs, stage 3**

The buyer's father and her boyfriend volunteered to replace the roof on the garage themselves, but I suggested that it might be better for him to wait until after the paperwork had gone through underwriting, just to make sure there were no additional snags. I knew that a loan can fall through at the last minute, and if that happened I'd end up with a nice new garage roof. That wouldn't be fair, and I tried to talk them out of it.

The buyers talked to the mortgage company again. They received assurances that "everything should be just fine," and they decided to go ahead and replace the roof immediately.

The materials cost about $400. Since they were doing the labor for free, and because this was a large repair that none of us anticipated, (it was definitely not on my to-do list), I offered to reimburse them for the materials at closing. It just seemed like the right thing to do.

- **Underwriting**

The roof was replaced that weekend, and the appraiser's report and all the other documents were sent to underwriting. Then, for the very first time, the mortgage officer hinted that the underwriters might not accept the appraiser's evaluation.

This was the first time that the loan officer had ever said anything about the loan that wasn't entirely positive, and it's possible that she was simply having a rough day. However, a house is never *really* sold (as long as a mortgage company is involved, anyway) until the underwriters sign off on the deal. I have had deals fall through in the last *week* before closing, for the craziest reasons, and I really didn't want that to happen again—after all, by that time almost all my belongings, including my books and art supplies, were already packed for the move.

While the underwriters did whatever it is they do, I spent the next few days online doing some research about appraisals. Sure enough, it turns out that it's fairly common for mortgage underwriters to question—or even reject—an appraiser's evaluation. This is probably because there was so much fraud going on during the housing bubble, when some appraisers would write down that the house was "worth" whatever amount he was given by a loan officer or real estate agent. Now, if the appraiser doesn't attach enough documentation to prove that recent sales can support the price he lists on his appraisal, the underwriters may reject it, and the buyers and sellers have to go back and renegotiate the deal.

- **Waiting**

There were still several weeks left before the closing deadline, but we had hoped to close early. Underwriters can't be rushed though, so we waited.

Almost 40 days had passed, and I had decided to move to South Dakota. I found a small rental house on Craigslist just a few miles from my daughter, and rented it sight-unseen. All of my belongings were packed up and waiting for the moving van, but I couldn't schedule the truck yet because we still didn't know when the underwriters would sign off on the loan—or even if they would approve the loan at all.

Now it was finger-biting time. With all my stuff in boxes, including all my art supplies, I didn't have much to do except wait and worry. My buyer was just as concerned as I was, and just as anxious to move. We had a steady stream of emails going back and forth between us, staying in touch and trying to keep each other positive while we waited.

Then on August 27 we received a call from the loan officer, letting us know that the underwriters had accepted the appraisal, and they'd be sending the paperwork to the loan officer that afternoon. We couldn't close until the loan officer to the the paperwork and then sent it on , to the escrow company.

The next day, the loan officer hadn't called so I called her. She said the papers still hadn't arrived, but she promised that she would get them the *next* day, Wednesday morning, by 10 am.

We didn't get a call on Wednesday, either. Even though we now knew that the appraisal had been accepted, the delays were beginning to get worrisome. My moving company needed some advance warning so they could schedule the truck, and I couldn't give them a date until we knew when we could sign off on the paperwork and I got my check. We had all hoped that we would be moving that week before the Labor Day weekend, but it didn't look like that was going to happen.

The loan officer finally called later that afternoon, but the news was not good. The underwriters wanted one more thing from the buyer. According to the loan officer, if she got that one last piece of paperwork, they'd be able to get everything to the escrow company by Thursday afternoon.

On Thursday, the escrow company called to let me know they had expected the paperwork from the mortgage company, but the papers didn't show up. It was now too late to get things done before the long weekend. We scheduled the official closing for the following Tuesday.

I called the moving company, and they assured me that a truck would arrive on Tuesday morning to pick up my boxes and take them to South Dakota. They actually arrived Tuesday afternoon, so I was moving my last boxes out of the house while the new owners were moving their boxes in.

As you can see, there were a few stressful moments during the 40 days between accepting the offer and actually getting my check. It isn't possible to either sell or buy a house without stress, but we all worked together to overcome any problems, and everything worked out just fine.

Would I sell my next house without an agent?

Yes, I certainly would. There was no point during the process when I felt we were in over our heads, or that an agent would have made the experience less stressful. There were no problems we weren't able to work out on our own, and all the same problems would have come up even if we had agents helping us.

As I mentioned in a previous chapter, I'm currently buying a house through an agent. Since I sold my own home just a few months ago, I can't help but look at my current home-buying experience from the sellers point of view.

When I compare the two experiences, here's what I see:

- My agent is a very nice guy, but he hasn't done anything that my sellers and I could not have done, either on our own or with the help of a real estate attorney.

- The sellers are paying my agent's commission, even though he didn't represent their interests. At several points during the process, my agent actually tried to talk me out of buying the house, and he suggested other homes that he thought were a better deal even after I made my first offer and we were waiting for the sellers' response. Since the sellers are paying my agent's fee, that doesn't seem entirely fair.

- My sellers will be paying almost $7,000 in real estate commissions when the sale closes. My own online marketing campaign cost me $22.

- The house I'm buying was listed for 12 months before I moved to town and I found the listing on Zillow.com. My own home sold 6 days after I put my ad on Craigslist.

That said, I know my own experience was unique, and I think I was really lucky to have everything fall into place so easily when I sold my own home.

Part of that "luck" came from the fact that I've been selling things online for so many years, so I understood niche marketing and I felt comfortable writing my ad and putting a website together.

Part of the luck came from the sheer coincidence that someone who wanted a house like mine just happened to find my ad the day after I posted it.

I was lucky because my buyer and her parents knew the real estate market as well as I did, and they weren't afraid to buy a house without the help of an agent.

And I was lucky because my buyer was already pre-qualified for her mortgage, and because she was so willing to work with me and keep me informed about her end of the process all the way through.

If this particular buyer hadn't been looking online on the weekend that I posted my ad, who knows how long it would have taken me to find another buyer? There was another person who called before I took the ad offline, but would he buy the house as quickly, or work with me as well as my buyer did? I have no way of knowing.

In fact, even if I did everything exactly the same way again, my experience might turn out very differently.

But still, if I ever *do* sell another house, I know I'll be selling it on Craigslist.

Building A WordPress Website

I F YOU'D LIKE to see exactly how I built the website that I used to sell my own house, you can find the instructions below. This is a simplified version of a multi-page tutorial that I previously published online, at:

BuildWebsiteEasyOnline.com

I wrote those instructions several years ago as a free resource for the artists who visit my sculpting blog. The instructions below are a stripped-down version for a very simple website, which is all I felt I needed to help me sell my house.

Buying a Domain Name and Hosting Account

The most confusing part about building a website happens right at the very beginning. You need two things:

- A domain name, and

- A hosting account

The **domain name** is the web address that people type into the address bar of their browser in order to get to your site, i.e. "YourHouse.com."

The **hosting account** is offered by a company that owns the computers, called "servers," that connect your site to the Internet.

If you want to build a simple website like mine, I recommend *Hostgator.com* for both your domain and hosting account. They have a great reputation for helping out if you run into a problem, and they're cheap. If you prefer to shop around, just do a Google search for "web hosting services," but make sure your hosting company offers a Control Panel.

Since I use Hostgator for all of my own sites and I'm familiar with their website, I'll use their site as an example. If you use another hosting service, they should have all the same options, although you'll find the buttons in a different place, and the prices will probably be different, too.

First, go to *Hostgator.com* and click on the big yellow button that says "View Web Hosting Plans." It's near the top of the page.

They have a number of different hosting plans, but if you only want a simple website, and (we hope) it only needs to be online for a few months, it makes sense to choose a monthly plan. Hostgator calls their least expensive option the Hatchling Plan. At the time of this writing, this service costs $7.16 a month.

When you hit the "order now" button, it will take you to a page where you can choose a new domain name. Hopefully, the one you want is not already owned by someone else. I was lucky, and "LaGrandeHouse.com" was available. If the first domain name you choose isn't available, the system won't let you register it. Try again with another name.

If at all possible, choose a short, easy to remember domain name that's easy to type. And try to get one that ends in *.com*. This is particularly important if you think you'll be doing any offline advertising in the local newspaper, or even if you want to put your web address on the for-sale sign in front of your house.

If you will only be advertising on Craigslist, though, the length of your domain name is not so important. The link will work no matter how long the domain name might be. However, for simplicity's sake, I still recommend that you try to create one that's short and easy to remember.

You'll be given an opportunity to add on some services, like Domain Privacy Protection and SiteLock. I unclick the boxes, to keep my costs down. My total cost, for the domain name and one month's hosting service, was around $22, but the prices are obviously subject to change.

After you've ordered your hosting account and domain name, your hosting service will send you an email with a link to your Control Panel. You'll need the password in that email, so don't lose it.

Now you're ready to start building your website.

Installing WordPress

Fantastico
De Luxe

There are lots of icons on the Control Panel, but the one you're looking for is the round blue **Fantastico De Luxe** icon. Click on the Fantastico button. It will take you to a page where you can install all sorts of programs. The one you want is WordPress, so click on it–it's in the column on the left.

In the right hand box you'll now see the **New Installation** link. Click on it, and follow the instructions to install a Word-Press blog on your site.

Be sure to write down the username and password you choose, and have the program send you an email with the username and password, just in case. You will need them every time you want to do something with your site.

The installation screen looks like the one on the following page. The first text box is already filled in with your domain name. The rest of the boxes will need some input from you, which I'll explain in the following list:

- **Install in Directory:** You want to leave this blank unless you have compelling reasons not to.

- **Administrator User Name:** This can be your name, or Admin, or anything else you want. It's best to use a name you can easily remember.

- **Password:** Don't use your birthday, your pet's name, or "password." You do not want your site to get hacked. Use a random string of numbers, letters and symbols, and write it down in a place where you won't lose it.

- **Admin Nickname:** You can just use your first name, if you want, or "Admin."

- **Admin e-Mail:** Just use the email address you normally use. Make sure you'll be able to read emails that get sent to that address, because you don't want to miss anything. If you forget your password, this is the email account that your new password will be sent to. You can change the email address later, if you need to.

- **Site Name:** This will show up as the Title on your new site. You can change this later, to anything you want.

- **Description:** This is the tagline that shows up under the title. If you change your mind later, you can easily change it.

WordPress

Install WordPress (1/3)

Installation location

Install on domain

```
lagrandehouse.com                    ▼
```

Install in directory

```
[                    ]
```

Leave empty to install in the root directory of the domain (access example: http://domain/).
Enter only the directory name to install in a directory (for **http://domain/name/** enter **name** only). This directory SHOULD NOT exist, it will be automatically created!

Admin access data

Administrator-username (you need this to enter the protected admin area)

```
[                    ]
```

Password (you need this to enter the protected admin area)

```
[                    ]
```

Base configuration

Admin nickname

```
[                        ]
```

Admin e-mail (your email address)

```
[                        ]
```

Site name

```
[                        ]
```

Description

```
[                        ]
```

```
[  Install WordPress  ]
```

Now press the **Install WordPress button**, and let it do it's thing. Remember to ask the program to send you an email with your username and password–you *know* you'll lose the slip of paper you wrote them down on...

Take a Look at Your New Website

Type your domain name into the address bar of your browser, and you'll now see your new website. There will be a header image at the top, which you can change. Your title and your tagline will also appear at the top of your site. You can change both the title and the description easily, if you aren't happy with them. I'll show you how shortly.

Your login page

The email you receive after installing WordPress will include the Admin URL, which will look like this:

http:// YourHouse.com/wp-admin/

WordPress dashboard

Go ahead and log in. You'll be taken to your WordPress dashboard. The dashboard seems to scare a lot of people, maybe because they remember back when building a website was really hard, and it was easy to mess things up. Play with things a bit, and you'll see that you really can't break anything. We're building a really simple website, so it won't even take very long.

Changing the title or tagline

It always seems to take me a long time to come up with a title that I really like. Fortunately, the title and tagline are easy to change, and you can change them as often as you want. To do that, click on the **Settings** tab on the left-hand column, and choose **General**. You'll see the **Site Title** and **Tagline** right at the top of the next page. Type in your new title and tagline.

If you don't want a tagline, just leave that area blank. You'll also see where you can change the official e-mail address if you need to, and you can set various things like date and time formats (which I simply ignore.) At the bottom of the page you'll find a big blue "**Save Changes**" button, which does exactly what it says it will do.

Since the title and tagline will appear at the top of every page of your site, you'll want them to describe your house and whatever unique features you want to emphasize. For my website, I chose the following:

Title–*La Grande House for Sale*
Tagline–*Urban Farm for Sale in North La Grande*

Disable comments

Under the **Discussion** tab in the **Settings** area, you'll be able to choose if people can add comments to the pages on your site. If you're making a site to show off your house to potential buyers, like I did, I suggest that you disable comments on all posts and pages. That way, your conversations with potential buyers will happen privately, by phone or email.

To **disable comments**, unclick the box beside "Allow people to post comments on new articles."

Plugins

Thousands of free plugins are available for WordPress sites. These plugins can turn a simple website into a really fancy, full-featured blog. However, for the purposes of selling a house, most of the plugins would simply make things more complicated. In fact, I only used one.

Several plugins come standard with WordPress, but they aren't actually turned on until you want to activate them. You can see the plugins when you click on the **Plugins tab** on your dashboard.

If you decide to allow comments from readers, you'll need to activate the **Akismet** plugin to prevent hackers from adding hundreds of spammy comments to your site. To use this plugin, you'll also need to follow the instructions for signing up for an API number. Since I disabled the comment feature on my site, I didn't have to do any of this.

You can also ignore the **Hello Dolly** plugin, which appears to be an inside joke among WordPress developers–it has no valid use.

The one plugin I did use was the **Lightbox Gallery plugin**, which makes the images on my site look really nice. It doesn't come standard, but it's easy to install, and it's free.

If you want to use this plugin, click on **Installed Plugins**, and then click on the **Add New** button at the very top of the page. Type "Lightbox Gallery" into the search box, hit the search button, find the link to the Lightbox Gallery plugin on the next page, (it should be at the top of the list), and choose **"Install Now."**

Widgets

If you would like any information to show up in the sidebar of your site, you can use the Widgets feature. You can use a **Text widget** for your contact information or a paragraph or two about the house. If you use the **Pages widget,** a link to all your pages will appear in the sidebar. If you use "Posts" instead of pages, you need put the **Posts Widget** in your sidebar so people can find them. Posts will not show up in the menu bar under the header, but Pages do.

You'll find the **Widgets** link under the **Appearance** tab on the left-hand column of your sidebar. A number of available widgets are shown in the center of the page. The widgets that are active are in the right-hand column.

Select the widget you want to use and drag it to the right. If there are widgets already in the right-hand column that you don't want to use, like the Meta or Blogroll widgets, just drag them back into the central area, and park them.

If you use a text widget, click on the arrow to open it up, and type in your text. Save it, and your text will now appear on your sidebar.

Adding Pages to Your Site

Now all the settings have been taken care of, and it's time to create a page. Since no one will see your site until you link to it on your Craigslist ad, don't worry about getting everything right. WordPress makes it really easy to go back and change things.

I recommend using **Pages** instead of Posts, because a link to all your pages will show up under the header graphic, which makes your site really easy for your visitors to use. You don't need many pages. One or two pages with photos of your house and a list of features, and maybe a contact page, is really all that's absolutely needed.

Click on the **Pages tab**, and choose **Add New**. Type in a **title** at the top of the form, and then start adding information in the large text box. Be sure to put as much information as you think your potential buyers will need before making the decision to call you. Even if your phone number is already in the sidebar text widget, you might want to add it again on the bottom of all your pages.

As you type your page, play around with the style options at the top of the text box. Try to keep things simple, of course, but go ahead and use the **bullet points** if you have a list–it makes it a list much easier to read.

Adding images

When you decide where you want your images to go, put your cursor in that spot and then upload your images. Images are really important on a website, so try to put them in a place where your visitors are sure to see them.

When I wrote the main page for my website, I put the price and address at the top of the page, and then added all of my images in a group. I then put a bullet-pointed list of features and my description paragraph below the images, so the pictures would stay *above the fold* (the area you can see without scrolling).

Images are uploaded easily, using the **Upload/Insert** button above the text box. Click on the image upload button, and then drag and drop images from your desktop, or click on the **Select Files** button and search for them on your computer. Remember to use images that are well-lit, and which have been saved for the web.

Once you've uploaded all the images you want to use on your page, you'll see them on a list. Click on the **Show** button beside each image, and label each image in the **Caption** area. You might label them "Living Room," "Bedroom," etc.

Then hit the **Save All Changes** button, choose how many **columns** you would like (I used 4, but it's up to you) and then click on **Insert Gallery**. This will place all your selected images on the page as thumbnails. Your visitors will be able to click on the thumbnails to bring up the large versions of the photos.

Preview your page

To see how your page will look to your visitors, click on the **Preview** button on the right-hand side of the Add New Page form. This will open a new window. Check for any obvious errors now, and click on the images to see how the gallery works. If you like the way everything looks, and you've checked for spelling and grammar errors, go ahead and click the **Publish** button.

Your page is now "live."

Setting the Main Static Page

We're almost done. The only thing we now have to do is get rid of that silly "Hello World" post that shows up on the home page of your site. You want the page you just created to show up there, instead.

To make that happen, go to the **Settings tab** and choose "**Reading**." At the top of the Reading Settings page, click on the button next to "**A static page...**" Your newest page will now show up under the drop-down box next to Front page, and you can click on it to select it. Click the **Save Changes** button and go take a look at your website. You should now see the page you just created, and this will be what your visitors see first whenever they come to your website.

Remove the silly stuff

To clean things up, go back to the Dashboard and click on the **Posts tab**, and select **All Posts**. The posts that appear on the list all came with your WordPress installation, and you don't need them. Click on the **Trash** link below the title of each post, and they'll be gone.

Now you can write as many more pages as you think your website will need. The title of each new page will appear in the menu under your header image.

Linking to Your New Website

Once you have all your pages built and you think your site is ready to go public, you'll need to let people know how to find it. You can add a link to your Craigslist ad, you can send it by email to all your friends and relatives, and you can include your URL (the domain name), in any print ad that you buy.

You can also add the link to forum and blog comments, on the sign in front of your house, and anywhere else that buyers might see it.

Remember—whenever you add your link to a website, blog or Craigslist ad, you must include the full URL**, including the http://** at the beginning. If you *don't* include the http:// portion of your domain name, the link won't work.

Some real estate agents don't put anything in their Craigslist ads except for a link to their website. I think this is a big mistake. I always give my readers a reason to click on the link. This is how I did this on my Craigslist ad:

See more photos and a more complete description at
http://LaGrandeHouse.com

My Website Details

I created five pages for my website, but a different house might need different pages and different information to show off its unique character. Comments were turned off, because I wanted people to contact me directly rather than converse publicly online. The pages I created were:

- **Main Static page**, with price, address, interior photos, and general details about the house, listed in bullet points. A very short, no-hype paragraph was placed below this list.

- **Yard and Garden page**, with exterior photos and another bulleted list of fruit trees and bushes that have been planted on the lot.

- **Market Research page**, showing comparable houses currently for sale and recently sold. (I found the listings on Zillow.com).

- **To-Do List**, where I listed the items that would need to be repaired sometime in the future.

- **Contact Page**, which was a bit redundant, since my contact info was also listed at the bottom of every page. However, I wanted to make it really easy for people to reach me, so I dedicated one page for just that purpose, just in case my readers looked for the contact page link.

Because I used WordPress, a link to every page appeared at the top of the site, just under the header image. I also used a Pages widget so links to the pages would also appear in the sidebar, and a Text widget so I could add my phone number to the sidebar, too.

Beyond Craigslist:

T HERE WERE SEVERAL things that I planned to do, in addition to posting my Craigslist ad. However, I didn't get a chance to actually try these ideas, because my house sold so fast.

Local Classified Ads

I did order a classified ad in the local Nickel paper on the same day that my Craigslist ad was posted. The ad didn't appear in print until after the house was sold, because I missed the weekly deadline. Nonetheless, I think it was important, because some buyers aren't familiar with Craigslist.

My ad was simple and cheap:

> *Small house, large garden for sale in north La Grande.*
> *$77,650. For details go to*
> *www.LaGrandeHouse.com 555-xxx-xxxx*

Even though the ad was very short, I was still marketing directly to my niche. I included the following:

- A short description of the unique features of the house;
- The neighborhood;
- The price (really important, in my opinion);
- The web address; and
- My phone number.

The "www" in the URL was not really needed, but it helps people recognize that you're trying to get them to go to a website. Since I bought my own domain name, the web address is short enough to print in a classified ad, and it's easy for people to type into their browser.

Zillow.com

I spend a lot of time looking at houses on Zillow.com, and that's how I found the house I'm currently buying here in Brookings, South Dakota. In fact, I gave them my email address so I would be notified whenever a new listing showed up on their site. Some of the listings I found on that web site were FSBO houses, but none of them were in my price range.

If I sold another house, I would put my "listing" on Zillow.com as soon as my Craigslist ad had been posted—just in case someone is checking Zillow but not Craigslist. They don't charge you to add your house to their site. To add your house, go to:

http://www.zillow.com

Do a search for your local area, and then put your cursor over the "Homes" tab at the top of the page. In the drop-down box you'll see "Post a Home for Free." Just fill out the forms, and your house will show up right alongside listing by real estate agents. Your house will also automatically show up on the Yahoo! Real Estate site, and may be picked up by other real estate websites as well.

If I put a listing on Zillow.com I would include as much information and photos as they would allow. I would also make sure that it was easy for people to reach me by including the URL of my website in the description of the house.

FSBO Websites

There are a number of websites that cater to FSBO sellers. You can find the ones that show houses in your area by doing a Google search, using the term "FSBO" along with the name of your city.

Some of these sites charge for a listing, and some of them are very difficult to use. Before deciding if it's worth my time, I'd try to see how easy it was to find houses for sale near my neighborhood. If the site isn't designed well enough to make that easy, or if I have to go through too many pages offering services (for a fee) before I find any houses, I wouldn't bother.

Some FSBO sites offer, for a fee, to add you to the local Multiple Listing Service. I suppose I would consider doing that if my house didn't sell quickly using free ads and my cheap website, but I would be very careful to read the fine print and see exactly how much the commission would cost before I signed on the dotted line.

YouTube.com

YouTube is now one of the largest search engines on the Internet. Many real estate agents do a short video of their listed houses and put them on YouTube.com, using the house address as the title of the video. Using the address in the title makes it easy to find the house on YouTube, and it also makes the video show up if someone does a search for the address on Google or Bing.

I put a lot of videos on YouTube, because I write how-to books for crafts, and the videos help me get visitors to my main paper mache website. To make sure my web address is a *clickable* link, I type it at the beginning of my video description, using the *entire* URL, like this: *http://LaGrandeHouse.com*

This is the same way that you put a link on Craigslist, as you recall. Also, don't put a period at the end of the URL, even if it's at the end of a sentence, because that would mess up the code and make it unclickable.

I always put my URL at the very beginning of the description below my videos so people won't have to scroll down to see it. I don't know if a YouTube video would help sell a house or not, but it would only take a few hours to make the video and upload it, so it might be worth a try.

WordPress Tutorials

This amazing system is constantly updated and improved by hundreds of independent programmers, who give their time and expertise to make it one of the best free resources on the Web.

If you want to learn more about WordPress than I could include in the previous chapter, you can find a wealth of information on the WordPress.org website:

http://codex.wordpress.org/Getting_Started_with_WordPress

About the Author:

J ONNI GOOD IS a craft book author, sculptor, and web publisher, who recently sold her home by using the skills and techniques she learned while making a living online. If you'd like to see her previous books (which have nothing whatsoever to do with real estate) you can find them on Amazon.com:

How to Make Animal Sculptures with Paper Mache Clay

How to Make Masks!

Endangered Animals Color and Learn Book

If you'd like to see what the author does when she's not selling a house, you can visit with her on her regular blog at:

http://UltimatePaperMache.com

You can see the Craigslist Ad and the simple website that was used to sell the author's home, at:

http://LaGrandeHouse.com

11099563R00067

Made in the USA
San Bernardino, CA
05 May 2014